麦格希 中英双语阅读文库

我是科学家

【美】比林斯 (Billings, H.)　　【美】比林斯 (Billings, M.) ●主编

李双福●译

麦格希中英双语阅读文库编委会●编

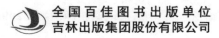

全国百佳图书出版单位
吉林出版集团股份有限公司

图书在版编目（CIP）数据

我是科学家 /（美）比林斯（Billings, H.），（美）
比林斯（Billings, M.）主编；李双福译；麦格希中英
双语阅读文库编委会编. -- 2版. -- 长春：吉林出
版集团股份有限公司，2018.3（2022.1重印）
（麦格希中英双语阅读文库）
ISBN 978-7-5581-4726-5

Ⅰ.①我… Ⅱ.①比… ②比… ③李… ④麦… Ⅲ.
①英语—汉语—对照读物②科学知识—普及读物 Ⅳ.
①H319.4：Z

中国版本图书馆CIP数据核字(2018)第046070号

我是科学家

编　：麦格希中英双语阅读文库编委会
插　画：齐　航　李延霞
责任编辑：欧阳鹏
封面设计：冯冯翼
开　本：660mm×960mm　1/16
字　数：220千字
印　张：9.75
版　次：2018年3月第2版
印　次：2022年1月第2次印刷

出　版：吉林出版集团股份有限公司
发　行：吉林出版集团外语教育有限公司
地　址：长春市福祉大路5788号龙腾国际大厦B座7层
　　　　邮编：130011
电　话：总编办：0431-81629929
　　　　发行部：0431-81629927　0431-81629921(Fax)
印　刷：北京一鑫印务有限责任公司

ISBN 978-7-5581-4726-5　　　定价：35.00元
版权所有　　侵权必究　　　举报电话：0431-81629929

前 言 *PREFACE*

英国思想家培根说过：阅读使人深刻。阅读的真正目的是获取信息，开拓视野和陶冶情操。从语言学习的角度来说，学习语言若没有大量阅读就如隔靴搔痒，因为阅读中的语言是最丰富、最灵活、最具表现力、最符合生活情景的，同时读物中的情节、故事引人入胜，进而能充分调动读者的阅读兴趣，培养读者的文学修养，至此，语言的学习水到渠成。

"麦格希中英双语阅读文库"在世界范围内选材，涉及科普、社会文化、文学名著、传奇故事、成长励志等多个系列，充分满足英语学习者课外阅读之所需，在阅读中学习英语、提高能力。

◎难度适中

本套图书充分照顾读者的英语学习阶段和水平，从读者的阅读兴趣出发，以难易适中的英语语言为立足点，选材精心、编排合理。

◎精品荟萃

本套图书注重经典阅读与实用阅读并举。既包含国内外脍炙人口、耳熟能详的美文，又包含科普、人文、故事、励志类等多学科的精彩文章。

◎功能实用

本套图书充分体现了双语阅读的功能和优势，充分考虑到读者课外阅读的方便，超出核心词表的词汇均出现在使其意义明显的语境之中，并标注释义。

鉴于编者水平有限，凡不周之处，谬误之处，皆欢迎批评教正。

我们真心地希望本套图书承载的文化知识和英语阅读的策略对提高读者的英语著作欣赏水平和英语运用能力有所裨益。

丛书编委会

Contents

Should We Blow Up the Moon?

Most people like the moon just the way it is. They write poems about it. They sing love songs to it. They hold hands under it. But Alexander Abian has a *scheme* that would change all that. He wants to blow up the moon!

Abian is a *mathematics* professor at Iowa State University. He has a bold

Buzz Aldrin stands next to the American flag that the Apollo 11 landing crew placed on the moon in July 1969. If you're set on visiting the moon, perhaps you'd better hurry. If Professor Alexander Abian has his way, the moon won't be around much longer.

引爆月球

　　桑普勒·巴兹·阿德里安站在1969年7月由阿波罗11号飞船宇航员插在月球上的美国国旗旁边。如果你打算也登上月球的话，那你可得快点了，如果亚历山大·亚比安教授计划成功实现，月球也不会陪我们多久了。

　　大多数人都喜欢我们现在的月亮。人们写诗歌赞美月亮，对着月亮吟唱情歌，在月光下牵手谈情说爱。但是亚历山大·亚比安却有着一个足以颠覆那一切的计划。他想炸掉月球。

　　亚比安是美国艾奥瓦州州立大学的数学教授。他有一个大胆的计划，

scheme *n.* 计划　　　　　　　　　　mathematics *n.* 数学

plan. First he wants to send some astronauts to the moon. They would drill a huge hole in the moon's surface. Into this hole they would tuck some nuclear *bombs*. After the astronauts are safely out of the way, someone back on Earth would push a remote control button. One second later, the moon would be blown to bits.

Why does Abian want to do this? He thinks it would improve the earth's weather. With the moon out of the way, he says, there would be no more *blizzards* in the Rocky Mountains. There would be no killer typhoons in Asia. Summer heat waves in New York City would end. So, too, would *droughts* in Africa. Not only would bad things end, but good things would start. According to Abian, the deserts and arctic regions would bloom. After we blow up the moon, says the professor, we would have pleasant weather all year long.

首先派送一些宇航员到月球上去，在月球表面上钻一个巨大的洞，再将一些原子弹放进去。在这些宇航员安全离开之后，回到地球的某个人会按下一个远程控制按钮。一秒钟过后，月球就会被炸成碎片。

为什么想这么做呢？他认为这样可以改善地球的气候。他说，如果是除去了月球，洛基山就不会再有暴风雪，亚洲也不会再有害人的台风，纽约市的夏季热流会终止，非洲的旱灾也会消失。据亚比安所言，沙漠和极地都会有鲜花绽放。这位教授说，在炸掉月球之后，我们就会享有全年的好天气。

---

bomb *n.* 炸弹   blizzard *n.* 暴风雪
drought *n.* 干旱

What does the moon have to do with snowstorms in Denver or floods in Bangladesh? Plenty, says Abian. The moon's gravity pulls on the earth. That tug keeps the earth tilted at a 23½-degree angle. And that's the problem. It is this *tilt* that gives us our seasons. The side of the earth tilted toward the sun has summer and sweltering weather. The side tilted away from the sun has winter and chilling cold.

Now suppose we blow up the moon. According to Abian, the earth would then lose its 23½-degree tilt. The amount of sunlight would no longer change with the seasons. It would be the same all year long. "*Perpetual* spring!" promises Abian.

So why haven't we blown up the moon? Most people like having it around. More than a dozen countries like it so much they have put

---

那么，月亮与丹佛的暴风雪或是孟加拉国的洪涝水灾又有什么关系呢？据亚比安说，这其中关系甚大。月球的重力吸引着地球，吸引力使地球保持23½度角的侧倾。这就是问题所在。正是这个倾斜角让我们有了现在的一年四季。地球倾向太阳的一面是夏季，有着酷热的天气；另一面是冬季，有的则是刺骨的寒冷。

假设我们现在已经炸掉了月球。根据亚比安的设想，地球即会失去那23½的倾斜。太阳光的热量也就不会因季节而变，而会全年如一。如亚比安所言，人们将拥有"永恒的春天！"

但是我们为什么至今还没炸掉月球呢？是因为大多数人都喜欢它的存在和陪伴。十几个国家甚至把它画在了国旗上。对这点，亚比安很清楚。

---

tilt *n.* 倾斜   perpetual *adj.* 永恒的

it on their national flags. Abian understands that. So he has come up with a second plan. He says we could try having two moons. We could "bring a moon from Mars." It could be put on the other side of Earth from the first moon. That way, its pull would balance off the pull of the original moon. Now the Earth would have two moons but no tilt!

There is another serious problem with blowing up the moon. True, it might *get rid of* the earth's tilt. But such a change might cause *massive* earthquakes. David Taylor of Northwestern University observes, "[Abian] would destroy civilization. But we'd have great weather." Thomas Stix of Princeton adds that most scientists wouldn't touch Abian's idea "with a 10-foot pole."

Such talk doesn't bother Abian. He wants to shake things up.

所以他又提出了第二个方案——我们可以尝试拥有两个月亮。我们可以"从火星带来另一个月亮。"它可以被置于地球的另一侧,它的牵引力会平衡抵消掉来自原来月亮的吸引力。这样,地球就会有两个月亮,却不会倾斜。

炸掉月球还会引发另外一个严重的问题。炸掉月亮确实可能会让地球摆脱掉倾斜,但这样的变化也可能导致强烈的地震。西北大学的大卫·泰勒说:"亚比安的方案会毁掉人类文明,虽然我们会拥有极好的天气。"普林斯顿大学的托马斯·斯提克斯补充说,大多数科学家并不会拿亚比安的想法当真。

这样的见解并没有让亚比安教授不悦,他想来个大革新。他质疑说,

---

get rid of 摆脱;除去   massive *adj.* 大量的

Why, he asks, do we have to accept the solar system the way it is? Why can't we move things around? Abian has some other ideas as well. He would like to change the *orbit* of Venus. It's too close to the sun, he says. Temperatures on Venus are a toasty 900°F. Abian thinks we should move Venus away from the sun. That would cool the planet and perhaps make it fit for human life. How does Abian recommend we move Venus? "We can shoot it with *rockets*," he suggests.

No one is holding his or her breath waiting for these things to happen. Even Abian knows that other scientists think his ideas are a bit strange. "I don't think [anything will happen] in my lifetime or in my children's lifetime," he says. "But I want to plant the seed."

为什么我们必须接受太阳系本来的面貌？为何我们就不能改变些什么？他还有其他的想法，试图改变金星的轨道。他说，金星离太阳太近了，它的温度足有华氏900度之高。他认为我们可以把金星从太阳旁边移开。那样可以使这个星球冷却下来，或许可以让他成为适于人类生息的第二家园。那么，亚比安是如何建议我们移动金星的呢？他建议"我们可以用火箭向它发射。"

不会有人屏住呼吸等待这些事情发生。甚至他自己都知道大多数科学家认为他的设想有些离奇。他却说："我不认为在我的有生之年或者我孩子的生命里，我的设想会成为现实，但我还是想播下这颗科学的种子。"

---

orbit *n.* 轨道   rocket *n.* 火箭

The Mysterious
Life of Twins

Jim Lewis was an identical twin. But he hadn't seen his brother since birth. The two boys were *adopted* by different families. They knew nothing about each other. Yet when they were brought together in 1979 after 39 years, something *spooky* seemed to be going on. For one thing, both boys had been named

Scientists have been exploring the relationship between twins for many years. They have studied pairs of twins who grew up together and other pairs who were separated at birth. They have come up with some remarkable findings.

双胞胎的奥秘

多年来，科学家们一直在探究双胞胎之间的关系。他们研究生活在一起的双胞胎和一出生就被分开的双胞胎，科学家有了惊人的发现。

吉姆·路易斯是同卵双胞胎之一，但自出生以来和他的兄弟就从未谋面。两个男孩被不同的家庭收养，因此他们对彼此一无所知。然而在39年后的1979年，当他们被带到一起的时候，一些神秘的事情似乎正在发生。首先，他们都叫詹姆斯，小名都是吉姆，小的时候，他们俩各自养的宠物狗又都叫托尼。

adopt v. 收养   spooky adj. 怪异的；不可思议的

James. Both went by the nickname "Jim." As children, they both had a pet dog named Tony.

But that was only the beginning. Each Jim had married a woman named Linda. Each then had a son. One named his son James Alan. The other named his son James Allen. Later, both Jims got *divorced*. Each had remarried—and in both cases, the second wife's name was Betty! Each Jim drove the same kind of blue car. Each had the same favorite drink. Each bit his nails, liked *woodworking*, and took vacations to the very same beach in Florida!

Could all of this be coincidence? Or do twins share a special connection? Scientists have long known that identical twins have the same genes. But no one believed there was a gene that tells you what kind of car to buy. So what made the "Jim" twins live such similar lives?

In the past, people thought twins were alike simply because they

---

但那仅仅是开始而已。更甚的是两个吉姆都分别娶了名叫琳达的妻子，然后又都生了个儿子。一个给儿子取名为Alan，另一个取名Allen，读音都一样。后来，两个人都离了婚，又都恰好与名为贝蒂的第二任妻子共结连理，两个吉姆都开同样的蓝色轿车，喜欢喝同一种饮料。两个人都爱咬指甲，都喜爱木工，甚至连度假都选择了佛罗里达的同一片沙滩！

难道这些都是巧合吗？还是双胞胎之间真有某种特殊的关联呢？科学家们一直以来都知道同卵双胞胎有相同的基因，但没有人会相信有告诉你去买哪种车的基因。那是什么让这对双胞胎过着如此相似的生活呢？

在过去，人们认为双胞胎如此相像是因为他们一起长大，遇见同样的

---

divorced *adj.* 离婚的　　　　　　　　　　woodworking *n.* 木工活

grew up together. They saw the same people. They learned to like the same things. But that is not the case with the "Jim" twins. They did not grow up together. They knew nothing about each other when they bought cars, named their sons, and picked out beaches.

In the 1980s a man named Thomas J. Bouchard, Jr., took a closer look at twins. He found other sets of identical twins who had lived apart since birth. Among them were Daphne Goodship and Barbara Hebert. Like the "Jim" twins, these women had not seen each other for 39 years. Bouchard *arranged* for them to meet in London, England. At that meeting, Daphne and Barbara showed up wearing the same kind of clothes! Both had chosen a light brown dress and brown *velvet* jacket.

As the two women compared notes, they found they were alike in many ways. Both had the *weird* habit of pushing up their noses.

人，从小开始喜欢同样的事物。但这两个吉姆却不是那样。他们并没有一起长大。在他们买车，给儿子取名或是选择沙滩去度假时，他们并不知道对方的存在。

在20世纪80年代，一个叫小托马斯·布查德的人对双胞胎作了比较深入的研究。他找到了其他几对从出生就分开生活的同卵双胞胎。其中有达夫妮·古德希普和巴巴拉·赫伯特一对，像吉姆双胞胎一样，这两位女士39年来从未听说过对方，布查德安排两人在英国伦敦会面。见面时，达夫妮和巴巴拉竟然以同样的装束出现，她们都选择了淡棕色的长裙和棕色的丝绒夹克。

随着两位女士的相互比较，她们发现在很多方面都有相似之处。她们都有向上推鼻子的癖好，都是16岁时在当地的舞会上与丈夫邂逅，都生了

---

arrange *v.* 安排

velvet *n.* 丝绒

weird *adj.* 异乎寻常的；不可思议的

Both had met their husbands at local dances when they were 16. Each of them had given birth to two sons, then a daughter. Strangest of all, each had fallen down the stairs at the age of 15. These accidents had left both twins with weak ankles.

Then there was Jack Yufe and Oskar Stöhr. Bouchard brought them together when they were 47 years old. It turned out that both men had short, *clipped* mustaches. Both wore *rectangular* wire-rimmed glasses. And both showed up at their first meeting wearing the same kind of fancy blue shirt. Jack and Oskar soon found more "coincidences." They walked with the same kind of swinging steps. They shared the habit of keeping extra rubber bands around their wrists. Both of them read magazines from back to front. They both even had the odd habit of *flushing* a toilet before using it!

The twins in Bouchard's study were more alike than anyone

二子一女。最奇怪的是，她们两人都曾在15岁时从楼梯上跌下，而且都是脚踝受伤。

还有杰克·于弗和奥斯卡·于弗，在他们47岁的时候，布查德安排他们见面。发现他们俩都留了修剪过的短胡须，都带金属线圈的长方形眼镜，在见面时都身着花式蓝衬衫。两人随即发现的更多的"巧合"。他们走路都迈着摆动的步子。都习惯在手腕上戴着胶皮套。两个人都从后往前看杂志。甚至两人都有奇怪的癖好，在方便之前冲洗马桶。

布查德所作研究中的双胞胎比人们可能猜想到的更为相似。他们在

---

clip *v.* 修剪
flush *v.* 用水冲洗

rectangular *adj.* 矩形的；长方形的

would have guessed. None of them had been in touch with his or her twin growing up. So what led them to make so many of the same choices in life? Some people think twins can communicate with each other in *mysterious* ways. Ron and Rod Fuller are identical twins from Dallas, Texas. They say each can tell when the other one is in trouble. Explains Rod, "There is a certain *bond* that we have for one another that I think all twins have."

Other twins agree. Andreina and Andreini McPherson grew up in Chino Hills, California. They say they, too, can each tell how the other is feeling. In fact, they claim, they can feel each other's pain. When one of them is hurt, the other one can feel the injury.

If that is true, then maybe twins raised apart can also communicate in special ways. Did the twins from Bouchard's study send each other messages for years without knowing it? Perhaps.

成长过程中从来没有接触或联系过彼此。那是什么让他们在生活中做出了如此之多的相同决定呢？一些人认为双胞胎之间可以以某种神秘的方式沟通。朗·福勒和罗德·福勒是来自得克萨斯的达拉斯的一对同卵双胞胎。在他们俩之间，当一个有难时，另一个就能知道。罗德解释道："我们之间有着一种所有双胞胎共有的联系。"

其他的双胞胎也都赞同。安德雷那·麦克弗森和安德里尼·麦克弗森在加州的奇诺山长大。他们说他们也能够知道另外一个人的感受。事实上，他们声称，他们能感到彼此的痛楚。当一个人受伤，另外一个可以感到伤痛。

如果那是真的话，或许被分开养大的双胞胎也应该能以某种特殊方式沟通。莫非布查德研究中的双胞胎们多年来都一直无意识地给对方传送讯息？也许吧。但或许终究是基因导致了这一切。1988年，大卫·特普里

---

mysterious *adj.* 神秘的　　　　　　　　　　　　　　　bond *n.* 结合

But it may be that the answer lies in the genes, after all. In 1988 Dr. David Teplica began to study twins. He took pictures of six thousand pairs of identical twins. He found some amazing things. These twins had *freckles* in the same spots. They got gray hairs at the same time and in the same places on their heads. Their faces got the same wrinkles. They even got *pimples* on their noses on exactly the same day! To Dr. Teplica, there was just one way to explain all this. Genes had to be controlling these events.

It's hard to believe we are born with genes that control when and where we get pimples. But that may be the case. Thomas Bouchard says his work also points to the power of genes. He believes genes explain many of the "coincidences" among the twins he studied. So who knows? Maybe there really is a gene that tells us what kind of car to buy.

卡医生开始研究双胞胎。他给6000对同卵双胞胎拍了照，发现了一些惊人之处。这些双胞胎竟在同样位置上长雀斑，在头上的同样地方同时长灰头发。他们脸上长着同样的皱纹。甚至他们的鼻子竟然在同一天长粉刺。对特普里卡医生来讲，只有一种方法可以解释这一切，一定是基因在控制着这些。

有基因决定我们何时何处长粉刺实在令人太难以置信。但那可能恰恰就是真相。托马斯·布查德说，他的研究也指向了基因的力量。他相信基因正好可以解释他研究中的许多"巧合"。天知道，或许真有某种基因决定我们去买哪款车呢。

---

freckle *n.* 雀斑

pimple *n.* 丘疹；脓疱

Is the Earth Alive?

Imagine drilling a hole eight miles deep. That's what Arthur Conan Doyle described in his short story titled *"When the World Screamed."* In Doyle's story, drilling that hole turned out to be a bad idea. As the hole got deeper and deeper, the earth began to *howl* in pain.

How can we tell that something is alive? It reacts to its surroundings, and if it senses danger it runs away or defends itself. It responds to food and light. It does what it can to keep itself alive. Can Earth itself be classified as a living being? Some scientists think so.

地球母亲

　　我们如何才能肯定地说一个事物是活的？它对周围的环境有反应，一旦察觉出危险，便会逃跑或自卫。对光和食物能做出反应，尽其所能维持自己的生命。地球可以被划归为这类有生命的活物吗？一些科学家认为是这样的。

　　想象一下，我们钻挖一个8英里深的洞。那是亚瑟·柯南道尔在他的短篇小说《当地球在尖叫》中所描述的。在柯南道尔的故事中，挖那个洞结果看来并不是好主意。随着洞越挖越深，地球便开始疼痛地哭起来。

howl *v.* 咆哮；号叫

Doyle's story was pure science fiction, of course. But some scientists think his image comes pretty close to the truth. These people say that our planet really is alive. It may not actually scream in pain. But it can and it does react to what we humans do.

The concept of the earth being alive may sound crazy. Most of us think of our planet as a kind of *giant* rock spinning through space. It is true that living creatures *swarm* all over this rock. But the rock itself is not alive. Or is it?

Dr. James Lovelock says it is. Lovelock is a British scientist. He calls his belief Gaia [pronounced guy-ah]. That means "Mother Earth" in Greek. Lovelock has written two books to explain his position. In 1979 he wrote *Gaia*. Nine years later he wrote *The Ages of Gaia*. "You may find it hard to swallow," Lovelock said, "... that

---

当然，柯南道尔的故事是纯粹的科幻小说。但是，一些科学家认为他的想象与事实真的很贴近。他们认为我们的星球是活的。它虽然不太可能因疼痛而尖叫，但它不仅能够也确实对我们人类的所作所为做出了回应。

说地球是活的，这样一个论调或许听起来很疯狂。大多数人都认为我们的星球是一块旋转疾行于太空之中的巨大岩石。的确，它的表面挤满了各种生灵。但地球这块巨石本身并不是活的。或者它是？

英国科学家詹姆斯·拉夫洛克医生说地球是活的。他把他的理论信条叫作道尔，发音为guy-ah，在希腊文当中意思是"地球母亲"。拉夫洛克已经写了两本书解释他的观点和立场。1979年他写了《地球母亲》一

---

giant *adj.* 巨大的   swarm *v.* 挤满

anything as large and *apparently* [dead] as the Earth is alive." Yet that's how Lovelock sees it. And he's not the first one to look at things this way. A German scientist named Gustav Fechner (1801-1887) thought everything was alive.

Fechner believed that all planets have a life of their own. In fact, he claimed, a *planet* is a higher form of life than you and I. As proof, Fechner noted that the earth doesn't have arms and legs. Why? According to Fechner, the earth doesn't need them. The planet Earth already has everything it desires. Human beings, on the other hand, are not born with everything they need. They must find ways to feed and shelter themselves. So they have had to develop arms and legs in order to do that.

书，9年后他又写了《地球母亲的年龄》。拉夫洛克说，你或许觉得要相信像地球这样巨大且明显没有生命的事物是活的还非常困难，然而那正是拉夫洛克的想法。而且，他并非是第一个抱有这种观点的人。一位名叫古斯特·芬切纳（1801—1887）的德国科学家认为一切都是活的。

芬切纳相信一切星球都有自己的生命。他声称，星球实际上是一种比你我都高级的生命体。芬切纳以地球没有四肢为据。为什么呢？根据他的说法，那是因为地球不需要四肢。地球已经拥有了它所渴求的一切。而人类却并不是生来就具备他们所需要的一切。他们必须想办法不让自己饿肚子，想办法遮蔽风雨。为了完成这些事，他们必须进化发展四肢。

---

apparently *adv.* 显然地　　　　　　　　　　　　　　planet *n.* 行星

Fechner's weird view didn't catch on during his lifetime. Other scientists simply ignored him. They went on thinking of the earth as a mixture of *lava*, rocks, water, soil, and plants. To be sure, these scientists said, the earth is a wonderful place. But it is not "alive" in any true sense of the word.

Then along came Lovelock. His bold views caught many people's attention. Even some scientists became interested in Gaia. Lovelock says Gaia is based on one key principle. It is this: Living things and the earth have a direct effect on each other. At first, that might not sound like a shocking idea. After all, it is clear that the earth affects life. There is no argument here. People who live in the cold mountains do things one way. Those who live in the warm *tropics* do

---

芬切纳的奇异论调在他的有生之年并未能够立住脚。其他科学家忽视了他的学说。他们继续视地球为一个集熔岩、岩石、水、土壤和植被一体的混合体。这些科学家们说，我们确定地球是个美妙的胜地，但从任何实在的意义上讲，它并没有"活着"。

之后，拉夫洛克的大胆理论受到了很多人士的关注。甚至一些科学家也对道尔提起了兴趣。拉夫洛克说道尔的设想是构建在一个主要核心原理之上的，即：生物体和地球对彼此都有直接的影响。最初那听起来并不是个多么令人震惊的想法。毕竟，地球对生命体施加影响是再明确不过的，这一点毋庸置疑。住在寒冷山区的人们以一种方式生活，住在热带地区的

---

lava n. 火山岩浆；火山岩

tropic n. 热带

things another way. Those who live in a desert do things a third way. So the conditions offered by the earth do indeed affect how we live.

But Lovelock believes the reverse is true as well. He says that life affects the earth. To show this, he built a simple model of the world. He called it *Daisyworld*. The main form of life in this model world is black and white *daisies*. The daisies grow when it is warm and die when it is cold. But if it gets too hot or too cold, the daisies can fight back. They can get the earth to change its temperature. If the sunlight is weak, more black daisies will grow. Their black *petals* absorb the sunlight. This tends to warm the earth. If the sunlight is strong, more white daisies will grow. Their white petals then reflect the sunlight, which will cool the earth.

In the real world, says Lovelock, the same thing happens.

人是另外一个活法，而以沙漠为家的人们做事的方式又是不一样的。所以说地球所提供的客观环境实实在在地影响着我们的生活方式。

但拉夫洛克相信这条真理反过来讲也成立，即生命体也在影响着地球。为了证实这点，他构建了一个简易的世界模型，被他称为"雏菊世界"。这个模型世界的主要生命形式就是黑、白两种颜色的雏菊。这种植物天暖时生长，天冷时死亡。但一旦天气过热或过冷，雏菊便会反抗。它们能使地球改变自身的温度。如果日照光较弱的话，更多黑色雏菊会生长。他们黑色的花瓣会吸收太阳光，这些光会让地球转暖。当日照较强时，更多的白色雏菊会生长。白色的花瓣则会反射太阳光，这样又会让地球冷却下来。

拉夫洛克说，同样的事情也在现实世界中发生着。人类和其他物种一

daisy *n.* 雏菊   petal *n.* 花瓣

Humans and other forms of life constantly cause the earth to react to what they do. Followers of Gaia believe that some of these reactions have been pretty strong. They say the earth has changed its temperature. They say it has changed the level of salt in the oceans. They even say it has moved *continents* around.

That does not mean humans have all the power. Lovelock notes that Mother Earth is one tough old lady. She can take a lot of abuse. After all, during her long history the earth has lived through ice ages, earthquakes, and volcanoes. The earth has even survived direct hits from *meteors*. It is not likely to experience anything worse. In light of what this planet has already endured, Lovelock says, a nuclear war would be "as trivial as a summer *breeze*."

Does this mean it doesn't matter if we blow ourselves up? That's

---

起不停地使地球对他们的所为做出回应。道尔的信奉者相信一些反映是非常强烈的。他们说,地球已经改变了它的温度,改变了海洋中的含盐量,甚至地球已经移动了各大洲的位置。

可那并不意味着是人类拥有着这些全部的力量。拉夫洛克把地球母亲比做一位坚韧的老妇,她可以承受大量残忍的虐待。毕竟,在漫长的历史过程中,她度过了无数的冰河时代、地震以及火山爆发。地球甚至挺住了一些流星的直接撞击,也不可能再会经受什么比这更糟的了。拉夫洛克说,与地球所经受的相比,一场核战争就像"夏日中一缕清风一样无足轻重。"

难道这就意味着如果我们把自己炸掉也不会怎样吗? 正是如此。道

---

continent *n.* 大陆;陆地

breeze *n.* 微风

meteor *n.* 流星

right. Gaia followers say that if this happened, the earth itself would go right on living. And sooner or later, some other form of life would take our place. Lovelock even thinks he knows what that life form would be—whales! He says whales have brain power far beyond what we have imagined.

Many people still think Lovelock and his followers are *loony*. Still, Gaia has a *magical* ring to it. The idea is catching on. There have been dozens of articles written about it. There have been Gaia lectures. There have been Gaia films. A 1984 book on Gaia sold more than 175,000 copies. No one yet claims to have heard the earth crying out like it did in Doyle's story. But maybe, just maybe, we're not listening hard enough.

尔的信奉者说，如果那真的发生了，地球自身会仍然无碍地生活下去。并且，迟早会有另外一个物种将我们取代。拉夫洛克甚至认为他知道是那种生物体——是鲸。他说，鲸有着远远超出我们想象范围的脑力。

仍有很多人认为拉夫洛克和他的赞同者们很疯狂。道尔学说却有着它的魅力，这种学说正在发展壮大。已经有数十篇相关论文被发表，以及有关道尔的讲座，甚至电影。1984年，一本关于道尔的书销售了175,000册。至今尚没有谁听到过地球像道尔的故事中所写的那样号哭，但是或许是我们听得不够仔细呢？当然，仅仅是或许而已。

---

loony *adj.* 疯狂的   magical *adj.* 有魔力的

4

Great **B**alls **o**f **F**ire

"**I** saw a great big shining light," said Betty Barrett. "It hurt your eyes to look at it." Frightened, she *rushed* to a friend's house. "I felt foolish," she later said. "If I hadn't [seen] it, I guess I wouldn't have believed it either. But it was the brightest thing that I'd ever seen."

We are all familiar with the sight of lightning zigzagging across a stormy sky. Some people have had close encounters with another form of lightning, but what it is and where it comes from is still a mystery.

神秘火球

对于一束闪电在风雨湍急的天空中曲折闪过的场景，我们都非常熟悉。一些人却和另一种闪电有过近距离的接触。但这种闪电究竟是什么？来自于哪还都是个谜。

"我看到一大团亮光。"贝蒂·巴莱特说。"看它眼睛都会受伤。"受到惊吓的她慌忙跑到了一个朋友的住处。晚些时候她说，"我觉得很傻，如果我没亲眼所见的话，我猜我也不会相信，但那的确是我所见过的最亮的东西。"

rush *v.* 冲；奔

MCGRAW-HILL

Barrett and her friend went out to look again for the shining light. This time they saw nothing. But just as the women turned to go inside the house, something *blew up*. They saw an enormous flash of fire. Then, just as quickly as it had appeared, it was gone. Later, the fire department checked for signs of a fire. It found nothing. Not a single *blade* of grass had been burned.

This happened in 1976 in Virginia. Seven years later a ball of fire entered a Russian jet. It was just four inches across. According to one report, it flew above the heads of the stunned passengers. When it reached the tail, it split in two. Then the two parts joined together again and left the plane. Mechanics later found two holes in the jet—one in the front and one in the tail.

In 1999 a Pennsylvania woman was sitting in her living room. Looking out the window, she saw the rain coming down. She heard

---

　　巴莱特和她的朋友再一次出去寻找那个光团。这次却一无所获。但就当她们正要回屋去的时候有东西爆炸了。她们看到一团巨大的火焰瞬间一闪。如它的出现一样，它很快就消失了。过后，消防部来人检查了是否有火烧的痕迹，却什么也没找到。连一片草叶都没有被烧到。

　　这是1976年在弗吉尼亚州发生的。7年之后，一个大火球飞入了一架俄罗斯喷气式飞机里，直径只有4英寸。据一个报道所讲，那火球从受惊的乘客头顶飞过。到达飞机尾部时，它一分为二。而后，两半又二合为一。火球飞离了飞机。后来，机械工发现了两个洞——一个在飞机前部，一个在尾部。

　　1999年，宾夕法尼亚州的一位妇女在起居室里坐视窗外，看到雨水

---

blow up 爆炸

blade *n.* 叶片

thunder and saw lightning. Then out of the corner of her eye, she saw what looked like a green ball. "It was floating about 25 to 30 feet above the street. It was about the size of a basketball.... All of a sudden, it grew brighter and larger and then burst in the air." Two minutes later the power in her house went out.

What was going on? What were these balls of fire that seemed to come out of nowhere? And why did they disappear so quickly? No one knows for sure. But stories like these have been around for centuries.

Usually the balls come and go within a few seconds and leave without doing any harm. But they have been known to *float* up chimneys and explode halfway up. And, as in the case of the Russian jet, they have burned holes through things.

These *weird* balls of fire are known as ball lightning. For a long

---

绵绵而下。她听到雷声看到闪电，随后见到了一种颇似绿球的物体。"它在距地面25到30英尺的上空飘移。大约有篮球那样大小。突然间，它越变越亮，越来越大，直至爆在空中。"两分钟之后，她家里便断了电。

究竟怎么了？那些不知道从哪儿冒出来的火球是些什么东西？它们又为何消失得如此之快？没人确切地知道。但是像这样的故事已经流传了几个世纪。

这些火球通常来去就在几秒钟之间，而且不会留下任何破坏的痕迹，但有人知道，这些火球曾顺着烟囱向上飘，并在半途中爆炸。并且，正如俄罗斯飞机事件中那样，它们也在物体上烧出了洞。

这些奇异的火球被认为是球状的闪电。长久以来，科学家们都对球状

---

thunder *n.* 雷
weird *adj.* 怪异的

float *v.* 飘动

time scientists scoffed at ball lightning. They said it didn't exist. Ball lightning didn't obey the known laws of science. So scientists thought it had to be just a *figment* of people's imagination.

Besides, there were many different reports of ball lightning. Some people said the balls of fire exploded. Others claimed the balls vanished without a sound. Still others heard a hissing noise. Most people said the ball lightning floated with the wind. But some people saw it go into the wind. Some saw it slip through cracks or go up the *chimney*. A few even saw it go through walls. Then there was the question of color. Some people said it was green. Others said it was blue or red or yellow.

All the eyewitnesses had been startled by what they had seen. Scientists figured that affected how people "saw" things. Also, there was the time factor. The balls came and went very quickly. Most

---

闪电的说法予以嘲讽。他们说，那并不存在，因为它违背了既定的科学法则。所以，科学家们认为那火球肯定是人们的想象而已。

此外，还有很多不同的有关于球状闪电的报道。一些人说火球会爆炸，另一些人声称火球消失时是悄无声息的，还有人听到了嘶嘶的声音。大多数人都说火球随风飘移。但一些人说它飘进风中，一些曾见它溜进缝隙，飘上烟囱。少数人甚至曾见火球穿过墙壁。随后又是颜色的问题。一些人说是绿色，还有人说是蓝色、红色或是黄色。

所有的目击者都受惊于他们的所见。科学家们认为这一点影响了他们如何"看"东西。同样，时间也是一个重要因素。火球来去得非常之

---

figment *n.* 虚构的事

chimney *n.* 烟囱

lingered just a few seconds. They never stayed long enough for anyone to study. Given this, it is no wonder that scientists responded to ball lightning stories with a sigh and, "Oh, sure. Right."

Scientists know that the eye can play tricks. People can "see" things that are not really there. Think about what happens when you look at a *flashbulb* as it goes off. The flash is over in an instant. But your eye still sees a glow from the flash. In short, you still see the light after the source of the light is gone.

Is that what happens with ball lightning? Some scientists think so. Ball lightning is usually seen in a thunderstorm. Normal lightning can act just like a flashbulb. It creates an *afterimage* in the brain. If you focus your mind on it, the afterimage tends to float around. It looks a lot like ball lightning. Also, afterimages last about as long as ball lightning. They have the same colors and shapes. And they

---

快，大多数仅持续几秒钟而已。不给人们时间去研究它们。既然如此，也难怪科学家们对火球状闪电的故事的反应只是一声叹息，轻描淡写地说句"噢，当然，的确"而已了。

科学家们知道人的肉眼会玩小把戏。人们可以"看"到根本不存在的事物。想一想当你看到一个闪光灯泡熄灭时会发生什么吧。灯光刹那间便熄灭。但你的眼睛仍能看到一缕热光。简言之就是，在光源消失后，你仍然会看见灯光。

难道球状闪电和那一样吗？一些科学家认为如此。球状闪电通常在雷雨天气中被见到。常规的闪电可以像灯泡一样，在人类大脑中产生一个后摄图像。如果你专注其上，这个后摄图像就容易维持而四处飘移。那看起来就非常像球状闪电。并且，两者维持的时间大体相同，他们有着相同的颜色和形状，都不造成任何破坏便消逝。

---

flashbulb *n.* 闪光灯泡　　　　　　　　　　afterimage *n.* 后像

leave having done no damage.

So is ball lightning just an afterimage in the brain? Many of the facts suggest that it is. But there are other facts that just don't fit so neatly. An afterimage doesn't *explode*. It doesn't make a hissing sound. It doesn't burn holes. And it doesn't knock out the power in a house. Also, how could the passengers on the Russian jet all have the same afterimage?

Scientists don't like to admit when they're wrong. But, in this case, they have done so. Many now accept ball lightning as real. They believe most of the reports are true. But they still don't know exactly what ball lightning is. There are many theories, but none that all people accept. Some scientists think it is caused by strange gases. Others think it is linked to earthquakes. Still others think it might be caused by small *nuclear* reactions.

所以说，球状闪电就是人类大脑中的一个后摄图像吗？很多事实都证实如此。但也有其他事实与此不尽吻合。后摄图像并不会爆炸，也不会发出嘶嘶的声响；不会把东西烧出洞来，亦不会导致哪座房子断电。而且，俄罗斯飞机上的乘客又怎么可能全部都产生后摄图像呢？

科学家们即便错了也不愿去承认。但这次，它们那样做了。现在，很多科学家都已经接受球状闪电为事实。他们相信大多数报道都是真实的，但他们依然不确定球状闪电为何物。有很多相关理论，但没有一个能被完全地接受认可。一些科学家认为球状闪电是由一些不明气体导致，另一些认为它与地震有关。还有一些人认为球状闪电可能因小的核反应而产生。

---

explode *v.* 爆炸 nuclear *adj.* 原子核的

In 2000 a new theory popped up. Two scientists suggested that ball lightning might be caused by burning *silicon*. Silicon can be found in soil mixture. When a lightning *bolt* hits the ground, it produces great heat. If the soil mixture contains the right amount of silicon, the bolt will release tiny bits of silicon in the air. The bits might then form chains in the air. The chains, in turn, could create puffy clusters that float. The clusters then *oxidize*, or burn up. If the heat of the ball is low, it will *fade* away. If it is high, it will explode.

The two scientists have not yet proved their theory. So in the world of science, it remains just a theory. But the existence of ball lightning seems pretty certain. So if you ever see this kind of weird fireball, you can relax. It's not your eyes playing tricks on you. And you're not crazy.

2000年出现了两个新的理论。两位科学家认为球状闪电是由硅燃烧引起的，硅可以在土壤混合体中找到。当闪电直射地面的时候，会产生巨大的热量。如果土壤中含有够量的硅，闪电便会释放极小的硅颗粒到空气中。这些硅颗粒可能会在空气中组成链条。链条便会依次地形成可以飘移的膨胀群团。这些群团然后或被氧化，或燃烧起来。如果热度不够，它便会消散；如果温度高，便会爆炸。

这两位科学家还尚未证实他们的理论。因此，在科学的世界中，它还只是个理论而已，但球状闪电的存在似乎十分确定。所以，你如果看见这类奇异的火球，不要惊恐。你的眼睛并没有欺骗你，你也没有发疯。

---

silicon *n.* 硅　　　　　　　　　　　bolt *n.* 闪电
oxidize *v.* 氧化　　　　　　　　　　fade *v.* 逐渐消失

Firestorms

Legend says that it all began with a cow. On October 8, 1871, Mrs. O'Leary's cow knocked over a *lantern* in a *barn*. A fire broke out. Soon most of Chicago was going up in flames. The damage was *immense*. Fire destroyed more than two thousand acres of the city. More than one hundred thousand

As deadly and destructive as this blaze is, it cannot compare to the fury of a fire storm. A true firestorm is so intense that fire fighters have no effect on it. It destroys everything and everyone nearby, and it burns until nothing is left to burn. Luckily, a firestorm occurs only under special conditions.

暴风火

尽管大火确实极具破坏性，但它却根本不能与一场暴风火的疯狂肆虐相提并论。真正的暴风火如此强烈以致消防员对其根本无计可施。它会摧毁周围的一切人和物，燃烧到没有燃料才罢。幸运的是，暴风火只在特定的条件下才能发生。

传言说，那一切都因一头牛而起。1871年10月8日，欧·莱利夫人的牛在谷仓踢翻了一个灯笼，一场大火爆发了。顷刻间，大半个芝加哥城都沐浴在火海里。所造成的损失惊人地巨大。毁掉了两千多英亩的城市地

lantern *n.* 灯笼

immense *adj.* 巨大的

barn *n.* 谷仓

people lost their homes. About 300 people died in the inferno. The Great Chicago Fire of 1871 shocked the nation. It became the most famous fire in American history.

And yet, on the same day, there was a fire in Wisconsin that was even worse. People did not hear about this second fire right away. The Great Chicago Fire was the hot news story of the day. Besides, the second fire took place in the small *lumber* town of Peshtigo. It took several days for word from this town to reach the outside world.

Peshtigo had seen plenty of fires before. Dense woods surrounded the town. Brush fires often broke out. The people of Peshtigo knew how to deal with them. This fire, though, was impossible to control. About 9:30 P.M., someone saw a dull red glow in the distance. That was followed by a low *rumbling* sound. Everyone in town knew exactly what that meant. The men jumped into action. The women got the children out of bed and dressed them. By 10 o'clock, the woods had turned bright *crimson* as flames leaped from

区，让几十万户居民无家可归。约三百人丧失了性命。1871年的芝加哥大火震惊全国，成了美国历史上最著名的火灾。

然而，在同一天，威斯康星州发生了另一场更可怕的火灾。人们并没有马上得知这场大火，芝加哥大火是当天的热点新闻。而且，这第二场大火发生在佩什蒂戈这个小伐木镇里，消息从镇上传到外界足足花了几天的时间。

佩什蒂戈已经受过了多次的火灾。小镇被密集的木材包围，小规模的火灾时常发生，人们也知道如何应对。这次的大火真的无法控制。晚上9:30左右，有人在远处看到一缕阴暗的红光，随之而来的是一阵低沉的隆隆声。小镇里的每个人都知道那意味着什么。男人们迅速行动起来，女人们从床上唤醒孩子们，给他们穿衣。等到10点钟，随着火焰在树与树之间

lumber *n.* 木材；制材　　　　　　　　　rumble *v.* 隆隆响
crimson *n.* 深红色

tree to tree. Sparks flew everywhere. Soon the *blaze* reached the town itself. The wooden sidewalks caught fire. *Sawdust* used in the streets to keep the dust down also burst into flames. The angry blaze *engulfed* one building after another.

There was no hope of stopping the fire. The people just tried to save themselves. Some sought shelter in large buildings. But as the buildings went up in flames, most of these people burned to death. Others drowned after leaping into the river. Three people jumped into a large water tank at a *sawmill*. But even they did not survive. The fire turned the water so hot that everyone in the tank died.

The Peshtigo fire destroyed every building in town. About 800 people died. That was 500 more people than the Great Chicago Fire killed. In terms of lost lives, then, the Peshtigo fire was much worse than the one in Chicago.

The fame of the Chicago fire is well earned. It was, after all, a

---

跳窜，木头被烧成了鲜红色，火花四溅。不一会，大火便蔓延到了小镇本身，木砌的人行道也着了火，街上用来压灰的木屑也燃烧了起来，愤怒的火焰吞没了一座又一座的建筑物。

要阻止这场大火毫无希望，人们只能忙着自救。一些人躲到大楼里，随着大火越烧越高，大多数人都命丧火海，另一些人跳入河里被淹死。三个人跳入锯木厂的大水池里避难。连他们也没能逃过去，大火把水烧得灼热，把水池里的人都烫死了。

佩什蒂戈大火烧毁了镇里的每一座建筑。大约八百人丧生，比芝加哥大火的死亡人数足足多了五百人。在死亡人数上比较，佩什蒂戈要比芝加哥那一场可怕得多。

芝加哥大火非常闻名，是一场真真正正的大规模火灾，但毕竟仍是

---

blaze *n.* 火焰

engulf *v.* 吞没

sawdust *n.* 木屑

sawmill *n.* 锯木厂

truly massive blaze. But it was a regular fire. The one in Peshtigo, on the other hand, was a rare kind of fire. It was actually a "firestorm." People who survived it talked of winds that were "tornado-like." They said balls of fire seemed to jump out of nowhere. These balls appeared and disappeared like lightning.

What is the difference between a normal fire and a firestorm? A normal fire is largely controlled by the weather. High winds can fan the flames. In fact, strong, gusty winds did help to spread the Chicago fire. Similarly, a heavy rain can *douse* a normal fire. For example, rain often checks forest fires. A firestorm, on the other hand, creates its own weather. It makes its own wind and rain. A firestorm can make rain fall and lightning flash even on a sunny day. It can create small *tornadoes*, or whirls, filled with fire and deadly gases. These little weather systems grow inside a *plume* of smoke

---

一场火灾而已。而佩什蒂戈的一场则是少见的。它实际上是一场"暴风火"。幸存的人们谈起来那飓风般的大风时说，火球似乎"jump out of nowhere"（像自己蹦出来的一样），来去就像闪电般迅速。

那么，常规的大火与所谓的"暴风火"又有哪些不同呢？前者很大程度上受天气所控。高速的风可以助燃。实际上，疾发的强风的确帮助了芝加哥大火的扩散。相似的是，大雨可以熄灭一场常规的大火。例如，森林火灾就总受制于雨。而暴风火创造它自己的天气，制造出自己的风和雨。甚至在晴天，暴风火都可以降雨打雷。它可以制造出填满火焰毒气的小型飓风或旋风。这些小的天气系统在空中飘浮的羽状气团中形成。

---

douse *v.* 插入水中   tornado *n.* 旋风；暴风
plume *n.* 羽毛；羽状物

that rises high above the ground.

Firestorms are rare. The conditions have to be just right to create one. First, the fire must be really hot. That means having lots of *fuel* such as dry wood, sawdust, *twigs*, or brush. Second, the winds in the area must be weak. A strong wind would blow the rising smoke across the land and keep a plume from developing. Third, the air must be fairly warm. Warm air forms currents that rise into the upper atmosphere. Cold air sinks. Cold air would press down on the plume and keep it from growing.

If the conditions are met, watch out. A *billowing* plume develops. It carries heat, smoke, ash, and gases higher and higher. Within this plume, the wind whips around at very high speeds. This wind turns into small but deadly tornadoes. The tornadoes can be as high as 400 feet and as wide as 50 feet. They travel at speeds of just six or seven miles an hour. But it's hard to tell where they'll go next.

　　暴风火是很稀少的。暴风火的产生也是要有一定条件的。首先，这个火必须是很酷热的。那就意味着需要许多的燃料，像是干材，木屑，嫩枝和柴枝。其次，区域性的风也要弱一些的。强风将会产生烟雾和形成飘浮的羽状气团。再次就是空气要保持一定的温度，热空气形成气流上升到上层大气层，冷空气下沉，在羽状气团中冷空气将会压低。

　　如果这些条件都具备，就要小心了！一个膨胀的羽状气团要形成了。它把热量、浓烟、灰、气越带越高。在气团之中，风以高速旋转，变成了规模虽小却可以致命的飓风。他们能达到400英尺高，50英尺宽。以每小时6至7英里的速度飘移，但会去何方无从所知。

---

fuel　*n.*　燃料　　　　　　　　　　　　　　　　　　　　　　twig　*n.*　嫩枝
billow　*v.*　翻腾

As the plume rises, moisture in the air starts to *condense* on the ash and smoke particles. This creates a cloud that looks like a towering black storm cloud. A 1993 firestorm in Santa Barbara, California, created such a cloud. It reached 38,000 feet. That's almost two miles higher than Mount Everest!

As the cloud grows, more and more moisture condenses on the ash and smoke particles. Soon rain starts to fall. In that way, a firestorm creates its own *rainfall*. The Santa Barbara firestorm produced lightning and almost half an inch of rain. But such rain rarely puts out the fire. One reason is that the plume doesn't stay perfectly straight. The upper part, where the rain forms, drifts slowly away from the source of the fire. So the rain doesn't fall on the fire itself. As a result, most firestorms don't put themselves out. They die only when their fuel supply runs out.

当气团上升之时，空气中水分会凝结于灰烟颗粒上，形成看似高耸的黑色沙暴般的云团。1993年，加州的桑塔芭芭拉的暴风火就是如此。它就达到了38,000英尺的高空处，那比珠穆朗玛峰还高出2英里。

随着云团越变越大，越来越多的水分凝结，一会便下起雨来。就是这样，暴风火创造了自己的降雨。桑塔芭芭拉的暴风火产生了闪电和几乎半英寸的降雨。但那点雨水根本不能熄灭大火，原因之一是气团不能保持竖直。雨水在上部形成，它慢慢飘离火源。所以雨并不会降到火本身之上。结果，绝大多数暴风火并不会被自己熄灭，只会持续至全部燃料都烧尽为止。

---

condense v. 浓缩；凝结   rainfall n. 降雨量

Dowsing: Fact or Fiction?

Ray Burbank was having trouble finding an underground water *pipe*. So he asked a friend named Henry Gross for help. Gross took a Y-shaped *twig* and held it in his hands. Then he walked back and forth over the ground. "The pipe's right here," Gross said at last, marking the spot

For more than 300 years, people have been using dowsing rods to find things hidden underground, such as metal objects, ancient relics, and—most importantly—water. Today, scientists are trying to find out if dowsing really works and, if so, how.

探矿术

三百多年来，人们一直都用探矿杖去寻找埋于地下的东西，如金属物，古代遗址以及最为主要的水。现今，科学家们正尽力确定探矿术是否真的奏效，以及它如何起作用。

雷·伯班克找一条地下水管时遇到了困难。便找了一位名叫亨利·格罗斯的朋友求助。格罗斯拿了一个Y字形的树枝握在手中，然后他在地上来回走动了片刻。而后，用一个木棍标出了地点，说："管子就在这儿。"

pipe *n.* 管   twig *n.* 小枝

with a wooden stake.

Meanwhile, the water company had sent its own men to find the pipe. When the men saw Gross with the twig, they broke out laughing. Still, even though they used fancy machines, they couldn't find the pipe. The next day, Ray Burbank dug up the spot Gross had marked. Sure enough, there was the water pipe.

Gross found the pipe by using the age-old art of dowsing. Dowsers claim they can find water and other hidden things under the earth. They simply walk over the ground while holding a forked stick or *rod*. Suddenly, they say, the stick or rod will *tremble* in the dowser's hands. It will point down toward what is hidden below the ground. When asked what makes the stick move, many dowsers shrug. "I don't know how it works," they say. "It just does."

同时，自来水公司也已经派遣了专人去找这条水管。当他们看到手拿树枝的格罗斯，都哈哈大笑起来。可尽管有着先进的设备，他们却无法找到那水管。第二天，雷·伯班克挖开了格罗斯所标出的地点。结果，水管真的就在那里。

格罗斯是用古老的探矿术找到的水管。探矿者们声称他们可以找到隐埋在土地之下的水或其他东西。他们就是拿着一根分叉的木棍，在地面上四处走动。他们说，棍棒会在手中突然间开始颤动，会指向地面下所掩盖的东西。当被问及是什么让棍子移动时，很多探矿人都肩膀一耸，说："我也不知道原因，但的确管用。"

---

rod *n.* 枝条

tremble *v.* 摇晃

Henry Gross is not the only dowser to amaze his neighbors. An old Vermont farmer named Milford Preston was famous for picking the best place to *drill* for water. One day a friend challenged Preston to a test. The friend dumped five *piles* of sand behind his barn. He told Preston he had hidden a quarter in one of the piles. In truth, the friend was trying to trick Preston. He had actually hidden quarters in two different piles.

Preston picked up a *forked* stick and went to work. He stopped over the second pile. He could tell a quarter was buried there. But to be sure, Preston checked the other piles. He knew right away that there was another quarter in the fifth pile. "You're not as tricky as you thought you were!" Preston *smirked*.

　　亨利·格罗斯并不是唯一一个让邻里震惊的探矿者。一位名叫米尔福德·普雷斯顿的佛蒙特州老农夫就因为择地钻井取水而闻名。一天一个朋友向普雷斯顿挑战。他在谷仓后卸下了五堆沙土，告诉普雷斯顿其中一堆里藏有一条动物腿。事实上，这位朋友想玩个把戏骗普雷斯顿，它实际上在不同的沙土堆里藏了两条动物腿。

　　普雷斯顿拾起了一个分叉的棍子，便开始了行动。他在第二堆土前停了下来，他已经可以确定动物腿就埋在这里。但为确保万无一失，他又检查了其他的土堆，他立刻就知道在第五堆土里埋了另一条动物腿。普雷斯顿笑言道："你并没有你自己想得那样狡猾。"

---

drill *v.* 钻孔　　　　　　　　　　　　　　pile *n.* 堆
forked *adj.* 有叉的；分叉的　　　　　　　smirk *v.* 傻笑

Dowsing goes back at least to the 16th century. That's when the first written account of it appeared in Germany. In those days, dowsing was used to find *precious* metals. The practice spread throughout Europe and, later, the United States. People in Asia and Africa also began to practice dowsing. Over time, dowsers have expanded their claims. Today they still say they can find water, *pipelines*, and metals. But they also say they can locate buried treasure. They claim they can find ancient *relics*, land mines, and dead bodies. Some dowsers even insist they can find objects just by swinging a chain over a map. The *chain*, they say, will pull their hand toward the right spot.

Some of today's dowsers have a pretty good record of success.

探矿术至少可以追溯到16世纪。那时,有关它的第一份文字报道出现在德国。那个时候,探矿术被用于找寻珍贵的金属。这项技术广为流传,遍布整个欧洲,随后又开始在美国流传。而后,亚洲和非洲人民也开始实践起探矿术来。随着时间的推移,探矿者们也拓展了他们的实践范围。现今,他们仍然宣称可以找到水,管道和金属,但也说能够定位埋藏的宝物,声称可以找到古代遗址,地雷和死尸。一些探矿者甚至强调,说他们只要把一条锁链拿到地图上摇摆片刻就可以找到目标。他说,链子会把他们的手引向准确的位置。

当今的探矿者们有着相当不错的成功记录。汉斯·施罗特是一名非常

---

precious *adj.* 珍贵的   pipeline *n.* 管道
relic *n.* 遗迹   chain *n.* 链

One of the very best dowsers is Hans Schroter. Schroter has spent a lot of time in Sri Lanka. He has picked sites for hundreds of wells there. In fact, he has chosen 691 spots. Only 27 of these have failed to yield water.

Still, the question remains: How do dowsers do it? What could make a stick suddenly bend down toward something far underground? Is there some force in nature at work? Some people think there is. They believe each hidden object must *send out* some kind of *mysterious* wave. Water, too, must send out *waves*. Dowsers, then, would be people sensitive enough to pick up these waves.

Few scientists believe in such unseen waves. Some say that dowsers' success stories are just a matter of luck. Others have a

---

了不起的探矿者，他在斯里兰卡生活了很长时间。在那里，他曾为数百口井选定位置。实际上，他共选了691个地点，其中仅有27个没能打出水来。

这问题仍然让人不解：探矿者们是怎样做到那些的？是什么力量让一根木头突然间就朝下指向某个深埋地下的东西？是自然界的某种力量在参与吗？有些人认为如此。他们认为任何埋于地下的物体都会发射出某种神秘的信号波，水也一样。而探矿者就是那些足够敏感，可以捕捉到这些信号波的人们。

几乎没有哪位科学家相信这种看不见的波。一些人说探矿者们的成功是巧合而已。其他人却抱有不同见解。他们说，并不是手中的棍棒在起作

---

send out 发送　　　　　　　　　　　　mysterious *adj.* 神秘的
wave *n.* （光、声等的）波

different theory. It's not the stick that helps a dowser, they say. It's the dowser's own knowledge of the land. Most dowsers are not *geologists*. They have no formal training in earth science. Still, they often know the land they are walking very well. So they might pick up *clues* without even realizing it. They might see that underground water changes the look of the soil in a certain area. The shape of the ground might offer *hints*. So, too, might the presence of certain plants or grasses. Geologist Jay Lehr says that experienced dowsers are often experts in picking up such clues. He says dowsers always "have an understanding, whether they're aware of it or not, of various surface clues."

Still, a few experts have decided that dowsing is for real. One is

用，而是探矿者自身的土地知识在帮他。大多数探矿者都不是地理专家，他们并没有接受土地科学方面的正式培训，但他们通常都非常了解所探测的那片土地。所以，他们可能在根本毫无察觉的情况下便无意识地找到了线索，可能会看出地下水改变了某片区域的土地外貌。土地的外形也会给予提示，一些植物或草的出现也一样。地理学家塔伊·勒尔说，有经验的探矿者通常都是捕捉到这些线索的行家。他说探矿者们总是"明了各种各样的表面线索，无论他们意没意识到。"

还是有少数专家相信探矿术是真的，其中一位就是德国科学家汉斯·

geologist *n.* 地质学家
hint *n.* 提示

clue *n.* 线索

the German scientist Hans Dieter Betz. In 1995 Betz wrote a report on dowsing. In it, he declared that good dowsers can indeed *detect* water below the ground. Betz is *respected* in his field. His report has caused other scientists to take a second look at dowsing. So far, though, most are not convinced.

So that puts us back where we started. Is dowsing fact or fiction? Tests have shown that it does work. But all of these tests, including ones done by Betz, have been challenged. Critics of dowsing say that every test has been flawed in one way or another. So dowsing remains an open question. Most scientists still reject it. But many people around the world practice it. Can they all be wrong?

迪尔特·贝兹。在1995年，贝兹写了一篇关于探矿术的报道。其中，他宣称出色的探矿者的确可以探测出地下水。贝兹是位受人推崇的著名专家，他的报道让其他科学家再次对探矿术进行了关注，尽管目前大多数都还是不相信。

所以那又让我们回到了我们的起点，探矿术究竟是真是假？实验证实它的确奏效，但是所有这些测验，也包括贝兹自己做的那些，都受到了质疑。探矿术的批评者说每一个实验都有这样或那样的缺陷，所以探矿术依然是一个公开的问题。大多数科学家仍然对其加以排斥，但世界各地的很多人们都那样去做。难道他们都是错的吗？

---

detect   *v.* 发现；探测　　　　　　　　　　　　　respect   *v.* 尊敬

7

Traveling Through Time

Imagine being able to travel 200 years into the future. Or think about taking a journey far back into the past. Time travel has long been a dream for many people. But is it just a dream? Until recently, everyone thought so. It was fun to *ponder*, scientists said, but it wasn't really possible. Now, some scientists are

This strange vehicle carries the hero of the movie The Time Machine forward in time. H. G. Wells wrote the novel from which the movie was based in 1895. But the idea of time travel has had a grip on our imaginations for centuries.

时光之旅

这台奇怪的车把电影"时间机器"的主人公载到了未来。电影是根据 H. G. 威尔斯写于1895年的小说改编而成。但时光之旅的想法却已经萦绕了我们的脑海足足有几个世纪了。

想象一下我们飞往200年以后的将来，或者一下回到远古时代。时光穿梭长久以来一直都是很多人的梦想。但是那仅仅是个梦想吗？直到近来，很多人都这样认为。科学家们说，那想象起来很有趣，但却是不可能实现的。现在，一些科学家在改变他们的看法。他们说时光穿梭或许是可能的，但仅仅是或许而已。

ponder *v.* 沉思

changing their minds. They say that maybe, just maybe, time travel is possible.

Think about time for a minute. What is it, really? You can watch the second hand on a clock move around the *dial*. If you watch it long enough, you'll see the minute hand move. And if you wait even longer, you'll notice that the hour hand also moves. The clock on the wall is one measure of time. But it is not the only measure.

A great scientist named Albert Einstein showed that time has many measures. As a young man, Einstein thought a lot about light and time. One day he had a thought that no one had ever had before. Einstein wondered what a clock would look like if he were riding away from it on a *beam* of light. He guessed that the clock would appear to stand still. In other words, time would stand still!

Why did Einstein make that guess? Imagine that a clock reads exactly 2 P.M.. You can see that because light shining off the clock

---

想一下时间，它究竟是什么？你会看到时钟上的秒针在表盘上移动，如果看得够久的话，你会见到分针移动，你要是再等久一些，便会注意到时针也在移动。墙上的时钟是时间的度量，但并不是唯一的。

伟大的科学家爱因斯坦证实了时间有很多种度量。当还是个小伙子时，他对光和时间思考了很多，一天他冒出了一个从未有人有过的想法。爱因斯坦心想，若是他驾着一束光线高速飞离的话，时钟会怎样，他猜想钟会静止不动，换言之，时间会停止不动。

为什么爱因斯坦会做出这样的猜想呢？想象一下时钟显示下午两点整。你能够读出时间是因为钟表射回的光展示出了表针的位置。光射到你

---

dial *n.* 转盘　　　　　　　　　　　　　　　beam *n.* 束

shows the position of the hands. The light travels to your eye and your brain reads, "2 P.M.." A second later, the hand on the clock moves to one second after 2 P.M.. Light is still bouncing off the clock. So another beam of light carries a new message to your eye. Now your brain reads, "one second after 2 P.M.." Beams of light travel so fast that you can read each message *instantly*. But imagine riding on the beam of light that carries the "2 P.M." message. The other beam of light—the one carrying the message "one second after 2 P.M."—would never catch up with you. So for you, the clock would always read "2 P.M.".

Using experiments, Einstein proved his guess was right. He confirmed that speed slows down the passage of time. In that sense, everyone has already done at least a *tiny* bit of time traveling. You have done it each time you have ridden in a car or a plane. Such

---

眼睛，你的大脑读出了"下午两点"。一秒钟过后，表针移动到两点过一秒的位置，光仍会从表针处弹出。所以另一束光线向你的眼睛送去了新的信息，你的大脑又会读出"两点过一秒"。光束的速度如此之快，你可以立刻读出每一条讯息。然而，想象一下如果骑上承载"下午两点"的那条光束，另一条承载下午两点过一秒的光束永远都不会追赶上你。所以对你来讲，时钟永远都会读为"下午两点"。

通过实验，爱因斯坦证实了他的猜想是对的，它证实了速度可以减慢时间的流逝。在那个意义上讲，每个人都已经进行了至少一点点的时光之旅，每次驾车或乘飞机都是。然而，这样的时光穿梭太微乎其微，人们注

---

instantly *adv.* 立即地

tiny *adj.* 微小的

time travel, however, is far too slight to notice.

Now think like Einstein. Suppose you go very, very fast. In fact, you go almost the speed of light. (Light travels at about 186,000 miles per second! That's more than a million times faster than a jet plane!) At that speed, you'd find that time really does slow down. Messages from other beams of light would *catch up with* you, but only after a long chase.

Because speed slows down time, you would age slowly as you *zip* through space. Meanwhile, back on Earth, time would pass as it always does. While you'd be getting five years older, people on Earth might be getting 205 years older. If you return to Earth after your five years, you would find you had traveled 200 years into the future!

Such time travel is not *feasible* yet. The fastest spaceships can go only a few thousand miles an hour. We haven't found a way to

意不到罢了。

现在，让我们像爱因斯坦一样思考问题。假设你移动得非常快。几乎以光速移动。（光的速度是每秒186,000英里！比喷气式飞机的速度还要快1,000,000倍！）在那样的速度下，你会发现时间真的会减速。其他光束的讯息会追上你，但要很长时间之后。

因为速度能让时间减缓，所以当你在时空中穿梭时，你年龄的增长也会变慢。而同时，在地球上，时间会以正常的速度流逝。当你长了5岁的时候，地球上的人们可能会变老205岁。如果5年后你回到地球，你会发现你已经去过了200年以后的未来。

这样的时光之旅目前还是不能实现的，最快的宇宙飞船也仅仅能够每小时飞行几千英里而已。目前，我们还没有找到一个方法可以飞得更快。

catch up with 追上   zip *v.* 给……以速度
feasible *adj.* 可行的

go any faster. In theory, however, there is a way we could do it. We could use what is called a black hole. A black hole, if it really exists, is a *gigantic* star that has used up all its fuel. It has *collapsed* into itself, becoming very small. The *gravitational* pull from a black hole would be immense. It would be so great, in fact, that everything passing by it—even light beams—would get sucked in. Things would get trapped in a wild funnel that looks a bit like a tornado. The winds in this funnel would be close to the speed of light.

If a spaceship could approach the funnel at just the right angle, the black hole might act as a *slingshot*. It could whip the spaceship around and send it flying back out through space at a super-high speed. (Of course, the pilot would have to be very careful. He or she could not fly too close to the black hole. Otherwise, the whole spaceship would get pulled in and compressed to less than the size

---

然而，在理论上，却有种方法可以达成。我们可以利用"黑洞"，如果它真存在的话。黑洞是指巨大的燃尽能量的恒星。它陷入自身，越变越小，来自一个黑洞的重力吸引力是惊人的。事实上，这种吸引力强大得连光线都逃不过。任何从黑洞旁边经过的事物都会被吸进去，被困在一个略微貌似旋风的巨大漏斗中，里面风的流速与光速接近。

如果宇宙飞船可以在合适的角度接近这个漏斗，黑洞会像弹弓一样，让飞船掉头把它以超快速穿过太空送出去。（当然，飞行员必须非常小心，不能离黑洞太近。否则整架飞船都会被吸进去，被压缩到比一粒沙还小!）

---

gigantic *adj.* 巨大的
gravitational *adj.* 引力的

collapse *v.* 失去自我控制
slingshot *n.* 弹弓

of a grain of sand!)

Now imagine that you want to travel back into the past. That would be even harder to do. You would have to catch up with light beams carrying messages from long ago. To do that, you'd have to travel faster than the speed of light. That is not possible. Nothing can go faster than a light beam. Still, some scientists think there's a way to get around that problem. They suggest taking a *shortcut* through space. That way, a traveler might be able to catch up with some old beams of light. Scientists have a picture in their minds of what this kind of shortcut would look like. They have even given it a name. They call it a "*wormhole*." No one knows if wormholes exist. But if they do, travelers might someday use them to jump back in time.

Before you get too excited about traveling to the past, think about some of the questions it would raise. Suppose you traveled

现在想象一下你要回到过去。那会更难，你必须追赶上那些承载很久之前的讯息的光束。那是不可能的，没有什么能比一束光跑得更快。不过，还是有科学家相信会有解决的办法，他们提议走条捷径。那样的话，人们就可能追赶上一些旧的光线。科学家在脑海里有了这种捷径的画面，甚至都给它取好了名字，叫"虫洞"。没人知道它是否真的存在，但是如果的确有虫洞的话，人们便可能在将来的某天利用它们回到过去。

在你为过去之旅而兴奋之前，先得想一想可能导致的问题。假若你

shortcut *n.* 捷径　　　　　　　　　　　　wormhole *n.* 虫孔

back to April 14, 1865. That was the day President Abraham Lincoln was shot. Could you prevent the *assassination*? Suppose you did. How would that change the course of American history?

Scientists often put the questions in personal terms. Suppose you time-travel back 60 years, to the days when your grandmother is a young woman. Your mother has not yet been born. If you somehow stop your grandmother from meeting your grandfather, where does that leave you? Now your mother won't be born. Does this mean you will cease to exist?

People love to *fantasize* about time travel. The question is this: can we really find a way to do it? Will it remain just a dream, carried out only in books or at the movies? Or will we someday be able to fly off into the future and back into the past? Only time will tell.

真回到了1865年4月14日，那天林肯总统被枪杀。你会阻止这场暗杀发生吗？假设你那样做了，那又会怎样改写美国的历史呢？

科学家们总是以私人的角度考虑问题。假设你回到了60年前的过去，那时你的祖母还很年轻，你的母亲尚未出生。如果你阻止了你祖母与你祖父的碰面，那又会把你自己置于何种境地？那么你的母亲便不会来到人世。这也就意味着你会停止生存？

人们愿意幻想时光之旅。问题是：我们真的可以那样去做吗？它会仅仅停留于一个梦吗？仅在书里电影中实现吗？或者有一天我们真的能飞向未来，回到过去？只有时间会揭晓答案。

assassination *n.* 暗杀　　　　　　　　　　　　fantasize *v.* 幻想

8

A Silent Killer

In 1979 Doris Goldman got a phone call she would never forget. It came late at night. "Are you Jack Toran's mother?" asked the caller.

"Is he OK?"

"Didn't anyone call you?" said the voice. "This is the *coroner* calling from Jackson Hole, Wyoming."

This man is having his heart tested for a rare disease that causes people to die suddenly in their sleep. It's called Long QT syndrome, and most people who get it never find out.

隐形杀手

这个人正在检查一种罕见的能在睡眠中突然置人于死地的疾病。这种病名叫先天性QT间期延长综合征，大多数患者都来不及知道就死了。

1979年，多莉斯·古德曼接了一个她终生难忘的电话，当时已经很晚了，电话那一端问道："你是杰克·杜兰的母亲吗？"

"他还好吗？"

那个声音说："没人通知你吗？我是怀俄明州杰克逊·霍尔的验尸官。"

coroner n. 验尸官

"Was he in an accident?"

"No. He died peacefully in his sleep."

The news broke Goldman's heart. She wondered how it was possible. Jack was a fine athlete. The 20-year-old had never been seriously ill. The day he died, Jack had been hiking with friends in the Grand Tetons. The doctors said his death must have been caused by the high *altitude*. That didn't make sense to Goldman. Thousands of other people climb in these mountains and don't die. Something else was at work here. But what?

Elsewhere, other young people were dying in mysterious ways. A seven-year-old boy died in his sleep. A 23-year-old died taking a nap. A 30-year-old dropped dead as she walked to get a drink of water after playing soccer. A 19-year-old nearly drowned while swimming laps in a *shallow* pool. A few hours later, she did die.

That was just the tip of the iceberg. About four thousand young

---

"他遇到什么意外吗？"

"没有，他在睡觉的时候安然地走了。"

这消息伤透了古德曼的心，她想不透这怎么可能。杰克是个优秀的运动员，20岁前从不曾有严重的疾病，死亡当天，杰克还和朋友去格兰德·特伦远足。医生们说他的死亡一定是因为高海拔的缘故。古德曼并不相信成千上万的其他人在那里爬山都安然无恙，一定是有其他什么东西在作怪。但究竟是什么呢？

在别处，也都有其他的年轻人在神秘地死去。一个7岁的男孩在睡眠中死去，一个23岁的年轻人在打瞌睡时丧生，一个30岁的人在踢完足球走去喝水时倒地身亡。一个19岁的年轻人在一个较浅的泳池游泳时险些溺水，在几小时后，她却真的死了。

这些仅仅是冰川一角而已，每年有四千名左右的年轻人无故地死亡。奇

---

altitude *n.* 高地   shallow *adj.* 浅的

people died every year for no *apparent* reason. *Weirdly*, they seemed to be in fine shape until the moment they died. Some were even top athletes. What was going on? Was there a link to tie them together? If so, what was it? For a long time, no one had an answer.

Doris Goldman was as stymied as anyone else. Jack's friends told her he had fainted earlier that week. This meant nothing to Goldman at the time. Most of the time, fainting does not signify serious health problems. The people recover and go on with their lives.

But a year later Goldman got a call from her daughter Sharon. Sharon had just had a *fainting spell*. Thinking back to Jack, Sharon and her mother grew nervous. Goldman began to wonder if the fainting spells had a common cause. She wondered if her children had been born with some unknown heart condition. A doctor tested

---

怪的是，直到死亡之时，他们似乎状态都一致很好，其中甚至有顶尖的运动员。究竟怎么了？他们之间有什么共同的联系吗？如果有的话，会是什么呢？长久以来，没人知道。

多莉斯·古德曼像别人一样处于困惑之中。杰克的朋友告诉她说，那个星期早些时候，杰克曾经晕倒过。大多数情况下，晕倒并不能说明一个人的健康有严重的问题，人们恢复之后会继续生活。

然而一年之后古德曼接到了女儿莎朗的电话，她刚刚昏迷了一段时间，想到杰克，莎朗和古德曼都紧张起来。古德曼开始思考是否昏厥有共同的原因，她怀疑是否孩子先天有某种不明的心脏病患。医生检查了莎朗的心脏，心跳慢而不稳，但那对一个像莎朗一样的年轻运动员来讲并不稀奇，她是一

---

apparent *adj.* 显然的
faint *v.* 昏倒

weirdly *adv.* 古怪地
spell *n.* 一段时间

Sharon's heart. The beat was slow and irregular. But that was not uncommon for a young athlete like Sharon. She was a top water-skier and runner. Sharon also had a problem with a *valve* in her heart. But the doctor said that was not a threat to her health.

In 1981 Goldman got yet another call she would never forget. Sharon had fainted while walking across her bedroom. Her heart had stopped beating. For a few minutes her brain received no oxygen. Sharon did not die, but she fell into a *coma*. She stayed unconscious for two weeks.

The lack of oxygen damaged Sharon's brain. She had to stay in the hospital for several months. After that she spent six years fighting to regain her health and strength. At last she did. It seemed as if all that hard work had paid off. Sharon took a *drug* to control her heartbeat. Later, she got married. In 1991 she had a baby named

---

位很棒的划水和跑步运动员。莎朗心脏的一个瓣膜也有问题,但医生说那并不会威胁生命。

1981年古德曼接到了另一个让她永远都不会忘记的电话。莎朗在卧室里走动的时候晕倒了,她的心脏停止了跳动,好几分钟她的大脑都没吸进氧气。莎朗并没有死,但是她陷入了昏迷状态。整整两周,她毫无意识。

缺氧损坏了莎朗的大脑,她必须在医院待上几个月。过后,她花了6年时间赢回了属于她自己的健康和力量。最后,她终于做到了,似乎一切努力都有了回报,莎朗服用一种药品控制自己的心跳,后来,她还结了婚。1991年,还生了个宝宝,取名为雅戈布。看起来莎朗的生活又正常了起来。

---

valve *n.* 瓣膜

coma *n.* 昏迷

drug *n.* 药

Jacob. It seemed that Sharon's life was back to normal.

Sadly, Sharon died in her sleep a few months later. "It was too much to have her come so far and then lose her," said Doris Goldman. The heart drug Sharon had been using was the right one. But her doctor had prescribed a dose that was too small.

There was good news, however. Doctors at the University of Utah had zeroed in on the cause of death. It was something called Long QT *syndrome*. The name comes from the long time between two beats (Q and T) in a defective heart. Long QT makes the heart beat wildly at times. At other times, it makes the heart stop.

Some people, such as Jack and Sharon, are born with it. But a person can *acquire* Long QT by taking the wrong medicine. Also, doctors have found out why only young people die from Long QT. In this case, it pays to be old. As people age, their hearts start to

---

然而，伤心的是，几个月后莎朗在睡眠中死去了。多莉斯·古德曼说，"花这么大力气把她找回来，又这样失去她，实在太可怕了。"莎朗一直服用的心脏病药物没错，但医生开出的剂量太小了。

然而，也并不是只有坏消息。犹他州立大学的医生们已经确定了导致死亡的原因。是一种称为先天性QT间期延长综合征，名字源于不健康心脏的两下心跳之间的长时间距。先天性QT间期延长综合征有时会让心跳过激，有时又会让心跳停止跳动。

一些人先天有这种疾病，比如说杰克和莎朗。但人也可以因为服药不慎而后天患上这种病。医生也已经找出为什么只有年轻人会死于先天性QT间期延长综合征。这里，年龄的增长是有好处的。因为随着人们的年纪逐渐增长，他们的心跳便愈发规律。所以，如果先天性QT间期延长综合征在一个人

---

syndrome *n.* 综合症状

acquire *v.* 获得

beat more regularly. So, if Long QT does not kill a person in youth, chances are it won't ever kill him or her.

Few people have ever heard of Long QT syndrome. It takes a heart test called an *EKG* to detect this rare defect. Even then, a doctor has to be looking for it. Long QT is very easy to miss. That is why so many young people died before *researchers* put the pieces of the puzzle together.

Even now, young people still die. That's because most of them don't get an EKG. After all, their hearts are supposed to be strong. And, in the vast majority of cases, they are. So doctors may think it is unnecessary to test them. Even those who are tested can slip through without having the defect caught. "Doctors miss it all the time," said one woman who lost her 19-year-old son to Long QT.

Most people who die from Long QT never know what hit

年轻的时候不能致死，那就很可能永远不会了。

很少有人听说过QT综合征。要想查出这种少见的疾病，得接受心电图检查。并且，医生要很认真地检查。先天性QT间期延长综合征是很容易查不出的。那也正是为什么那么多年轻人在科研人员拭清疑云查出原因之前就丧命了。

甚至现在，一直都有很多年轻人死亡。因为他们大都不去作心电图检查。毕竟，他们的心脏被认为是很健康的。并且大多数人的确如此。所以医生们便认为没必要兴师动众地检查年轻的人们。即使那些参加检查的，疾病也可能逃过检查。一位妇女19岁的儿子就死于先天性QT间期延长综合征，她说，"医生总是会误诊遗落掉疾病。"

绝大多数死于先天性QT间期延长综合征的人们都不知道是什么夺走了他们的生命。其实会有一些先兆。晕厥就意味着有事情不对劲。感觉头脑发

EKG *abbr.* 心电图　　　　　　　　　　researcher *n.* 研究员

them. There may be some warning signs. Fainting may mean that something is wrong. Feeling light in the head can be a danger signal. But some people have no warning at all. One day they just drop dead.Their hearts are like time *bombs* waiting to go off. The fatal trigger can be exercise such as swimming or running. Or it can be a shock as simple as a surprise doorbell ring. One woman died when a two-year-old darted past her down an *aisle* in church. Death can even be *triggered* by the stress of a bad dream.

Doris Goldman's hunch was right. Jack and Sharon were born with Long QT. She checked the heart records of her family back as far as she could. She discovered that 21 members of her family had

飘是个很危险的信号。但一些人全然没有警惕性。而某一天就倒地身亡。他们的心脏就像随时等待爆发的定时炸弹一样。而致命的扳机就可能是像游泳、跑步一样的运动, 也可能是像突然间的门铃一样简单的惊吓。一个女人在教堂里, 一个两岁大的小孩子在过道上从她身边急冲跑过时, 她便死了。死亡也可能就因一个噩梦而来。

多莉斯·古德曼的预感是对的。杰克和莎朗就是先天患有先天性QT间期延长综合征。她尽可能往前检查了她家族的心脏病史。发现在她家里有21位成员都患有先天性QT间期延长综合征, 包括她自身。她唯一活着的女儿南

bomb *n.* 炸弹
trigger *v.* 引发

aisle *n.* 通道

Long QT. She had it herself. So, too, did her one living daughter, Nancy. Sharon's young son, Jacob, was also born with it. But, luckily, they now knew it. With the right treatment, Jacob should be OK.

Goldman started a *campaign* to teach victims as well as doctors about Long QT. She called the heart defect "a silent killer." But it doesn't have to be a killer. While there is no cure, there are drugs to treat it. So, if someone has a family history of sudden death, he or she should get an EKG. It could save a life.

Goldman's campaign has helped give meaning to the deaths of Jack and Sharon. "I stay sane because I can help someone else," she once said. "No other family should have to go through what we've been through. The only way for me to go on was to take a tragedy and turn it into a *mission*."

茜也一样。莎朗幼小的儿子雅戈布也患有该病。但幸运的是，他们现在知道了。如果接受适当的治疗，雅戈布就会安然无恙。

古德曼发起了一项运动，向患者们以及医生们宣传如何防治先天性QT间期延长综合征。 她管这种心脏病称为"无声的杀手"。但它不见得肯定能成为"杀手"。即使没有痊愈的疗法，但有药物可以治疗。所以，如果谁的家族史上有猝死的先例，他就应该做一次心电图检查了。那可以挽救一条性命。

古德曼的运动给杰克和莎朗的死去赋予了一定的意义。她曾经说，"我还保持着神态清醒，因为我还可以帮助其他人。不要再让任何别的家庭遭受我所经受的这一切了。我唯一的方法就是面对并且承担下这个悲剧，把它转变为一个任务。"

campaign *n.* 运动　　　　　　　　mission *n.* 任务

The Healing Power of Maggots

Have you ever opened a *garbage* pail and found *maggots* swarming around inside? How did you feel? Were you *grossed out*? Did these wriggling little bugs make you sick to your stomach? These creatures are pretty *disgusting*. But hold on. Maggots might not really be so creepy after all. In fact, they could save your life!

Maggots are an early stage of flies. They look like little worms and they eat constantly. Recently, doctors have rediscovered what many ancient healers knew. Because maggots have such a huge appetite for decayed flesh, they can be good medicine!

蛆虫的疗效

蛆虫是苍蝇的幼虫。它们看起来像小虫子，一直不停地吃。近来，医生们又发现许多古代行医者所了解的事情。蛆虫可以是极好的疗伤药。因为它们对腐烂的血肉有着极好的胃口。

你可曾打开过一个垃圾桶，然后看到里面拥满蛆虫的情形？感觉怎样？是否反感得不行？这些小蠕虫是否让你恶心到了极点？这些生物的确很令人作呕。然而，蛆虫并不是那样糟糕。实际上，它们可以挽救一个人的生命。

garbage *n.* 垃圾
gross out 惹人讨厌

maggot *n.* 蛆
disgust *v.* 厌恶

Maggots are the larvae of flies. Flies start out as eggs. Adult female flies often lay their eggs on food, garbage, rotting plants, or dead animals. These eggs look like tiny *grains* of rice. In a couple of days, the eggs hatch and out crawl the maggots. These maggots are *pale* yellow or white. They spend most of their time eating. After a few days, the growing maggots reach the point where they turn into flies.

It's the eating habits of maggots that make them so helpful. Doctors discovered this during World War I. Wounded soldiers were often *stranded* on the *battlefield* for hours and even days. In some cases, their open wounds remained clear. In other cases, their wounds became filled with hundreds of maggots. Doctors found that the soldiers with clear wounds often died. The wounds became infected, sending poison surging through the body. It was the infection more than the wounds themselves that killed these men.

蛆是苍蝇的幼虫。蝇是从卵的形态开始发育的。雌性成虫经常把卵产生在食物上，垃圾上，腐烂的植物上或动物的尸体上。这些卵看起来就像小的米粒一样。几天后，卵就会孵化并爬出蛆虫来。蛆是淡黄色或白色的，他们大多数时间都在吃东西。几天后，这些一直不停地生长的蛆虫便会变为苍蝇。

是他们饮食习惯让蛆如此有用。一战期间，医生们就已经发现了这点。受伤的战士们经常几小时甚至几天地受困于战场上。有时候，未被包扎的伤口上也没有，有时上面爬满了成百上千的蛆。医生们发现第一种情况的战士常常都会死掉。他们的伤口会感染，把病毒扩散到全身。实际上是感染而不是伤口本身夺取了这些人的生命。

---

grain *n.* 粮食

strand *v.* 使陷于困境

pale *adj.* 暗淡的

battlefield *n.* 战场

But those soldiers with swarming maggots in their wounds had a better *record*. Many of them survived! Why? The maggots were little eating machines. They constantly searched the wounds for food. Luckily, these maggots had no desire to eat healthy flesh. They craved only *decayed* flesh and *pus*. By eating up the rotten parts of a person's body, they helped to prevent *infection*. In this way, they saved many lives. The maggots helped in other ways, as well. They released a chemical that killed the germs they didn't eat. Also, by crawling over the good flesh, they gave it a healthy massage.

After the war, doctors began to study maggots. They found some interesting things. First, the use of maggots to heal wounds was not really new. It goes back a long way. The Maya peoples of Mexico used maggots more than a thousand years ago. In the 1500s, a French doctor named Ambroise Paré noticed maggots in wounds. He felt at the time that the maggots might be doing some good.

　　然而那些伤口爬满蛆虫的战士们情况好很多。有很多都存活了下来！为什么会这样？蛆是小型的觅食机器。它们停在伤口上寻找食物。幸运的是，这些蛆虫对健康未腐的血肉并不感兴趣，而只钟爱已经腐烂的肉和脓液。它们吃净一个人身体上已腐烂的部分，也就帮他防止了感染。通过这种方式，蛆虫挽救了很多人的性命。它们也以其他方式起作用，释放出的化学物可以杀掉它们没吃的那些细菌。同样，蛆虫在好的血肉上爬来爬去，也就提供了有益健康的按摩。

　　战后，医生们开始研究蛆虫。他们发现一些有趣的事。首先，用蛆虫疗伤并不是近来的事，而要追溯到很久以前。墨西哥的玛雅人在一千多年前就使用蛆虫了。在16世纪，一位名叫安布洛斯·帕雷的法国医生注意到

---

record *n.* 记录
pus *n.* 脓液

decay *v.* 腐烂
infection. *n.* 感染

Later, Baron D. J. Larrey, another French doctor, praised the work of maggots. He noted that most soldiers were terrified when they saw maggots in their wounds. The soldiers *calmed down* only when they saw the good these creatures did.

By the 1930s, doctors were using maggots as a standard *treatment*. Drug companies bred maggots and sold them to hospitals. The maggots all came from blow flies. (Maggots from other flies had to be avoided. They would eat healthy flesh!) An average wound needed about 500 maggots. These maggots would finish their job in two to five days. Then they would turn into flies and fly away.

The use of maggots ended in the 1940s. New wonder drugs took their place. At the time, people were very excited about these drugs. The drugs were neat and clean and easy to use. They were much more *appealing to* patients. Doctors, too, found them more pleasant to use.

了伤口中的蛆虫。当时他就认为这些蛆虫会有帮助。后来，另一位法国医生巴伦·D. J. 拉里赞赏了蛆虫的功用。他注意到大多数士兵在看到他们的伤口中有蛆时都吓坏了。当了解这些生物所做的好事时才平静下来。

到20世纪30年代，医生们已经把蛆虫当作一种标准疗法来使用了。医药公司养殖蛆虫，卖给医院。这些蛆虫全部来自绿头苍蝇。（其他品种苍蝇的蛆要避免，因为他们会吃好的肌肉。）平均一个伤口需要大约五百只蛆虫，它们会用2到5天完成工作，然后变成苍蝇飞走。

对蛆虫的使用在20世纪40年代时结束，新的特效药取代了它的位置。当时，人们为这些药品的出现而非常兴奋。这些药品既清洁又实用，对病人来讲更具吸引力，更容易接受。医生们他发现这些药品使用起来更称心。

---

calm down 镇定下来   treatment *n.* 疗法
appeal to 对……有吸引力

It is easy to understand why people would prefer drugs to maggots. But was this good science? The new drugs were very expensive. And as it turned out, they didn't always work that well. By the 1990s, doctors were *rethinking* their position. said Dr. Jane Petro, "Maggots are more effective and cheaper than a lot of [costly wonder drugs]." Also, maggots are really good at healing tough bone infections. That's because bones have few blood *vessels*. Modern drugs, which travel through the bloodstream, can't reach these infections.

And so the lowly maggot has been making a *mild* comeback. Recently a few doctors have started to use them again. Take the case of Dr. Grady Dugas. One of his patients developed deep *sores*. The sores got infected. They were especially bad on the patient's feet. Dr. Dugas tried using some wonder drugs to clear the sores.

很容易理解为什么人们相对于蛆虫来讲更喜欢药品，但实际上呢？新药品非常昂贵，而且疗效并不总是那样好。到20世纪90年代，医生们又重新给药品定位了。简·佩罗医生说："蛆虫比很多昂贵的特效药都更有效更实惠。"同样，蛆虫在治疗严重的骨感染方面也非常地有效。因为骨上几乎没有血管。现代药品都是通过血液扩散而作用的，所以到达不了骨上的感染处。

所以，便宜的蛆虫又在渐渐地回潮。最近，一些医生又在运用它们了。以格雷迪·杜加斯医生为例。他的一位病人有剧烈的疾痛。他的伤处已经感染，病人的双脚病情尤为严重。杜加斯医生尝试了一些特效药来镇痛，可没

---

rethink *v.* 重新考虑   vessel *n.* 血管

mild *adj.* 轻微的   sore *n.* 痛处

None of the drugs seemed to do any good. He then tried surgery to remove the infected tissue. That didn't work either.

Dr. Dugas felt he might have to *amputate* the patient's feet. Then he remembered his grandmother. She had suffered from sores back in the 1930s. Her doctors had treated the sores with maggots. Dugas recalled that the maggots had healed the sores. So he ordered a supply of blow fly eggs. He placed them in his patient's sores. The eggs hatched, and the maggots went to work. They *wiped out* the infection, and the sores healed. The maggots had saved the patient's feet!

Still, maggots aren't as popular as they could be. Some doctors remain *squeamish* about using them. And, remember, maggots turn into flies. Not many people want to walk into a hospital filled with flies. So the healing power of maggots remains a well-kept secret. As Dr. Petro put it, "It just goes back to the disgust factor."

有一种奏效。然后他又通过手术切除了受到感染的组织，但也并不起作用。

杜加斯医生认为他或许应该给这位病人截去双脚。可他想起了他的祖母。她曾在20世纪30年代受过剧痛之苦。当时，她的医生采用蛆虫治疗。杜加斯记得蛆虫的确治愈了祖母的病痛。所以他也订了一定量的绿蝇卵，把它们放在那位病人的痛处。卵孵化了，蛆虫也开始工作。他们消除了感染，痛处愈合了。蛆虫挽救了病人的双脚。

可蛆虫仍然没有受到应得重视，一些医生仍对它们排斥。而且，不要忘了，蛆是会变成苍蝇的。没有很多人会想走进一家飞满苍蝇的医院。所以，蛆虫的治疗能力仍是一个保守得很好的秘密。正像德特罗医生说得那样，"又回到蛆虫恶心人的那一方面上去了。"

---

amputate *v.* 截肢   wipe out 消灭
squeamish *adj.* 诚实谨慎的；正派的

10

Psychics Who Solve Crimes

On December 3, 1967, Dorothy Allison had a frightening dream. In it, she saw the body of a small boy in a river. Allison tried to forget about the dream. But she couldn't. At last she called the police in her town of Nutley, New Jersey. It *turned out* that a five-year-old boy had

Some people claim that they can "see" events that happen far away from them. These people, called psychics, can't explain how they obtain their information. But what they know may give clues to police stumped by mysterious crimes.

灵媒侦探

一些人声称他们可以"看到"发生在千里之外的事情。这些"灵异人士"也不能解释他们是如何获得这些信息的。然而，他们的所知却很可能为因神秘案件而困扰不堪的警方提供线索。

1967年12月3日，多萝西·阿里森做了一个可怕的梦。梦里，她在一条河中看到一个小男孩的尸体，阿里森试图忘掉这个梦，可她做不到。最后还是给所在的纳特利镇的警局打了电话，结果发现真的有一个5岁小男

turn out　结果是；证明是

indeed drowned in a local river. But he had fallen into the water two hours after Dorothy Allison's dream.

When Allison called the police, they were still looking for the boy's body. They did not want to be bothered by *housewives* with wild dreams. The tragedy had been reported in the newspapers. So police figured Allison had learned about it there. But Dorothy Allison knew things that had not been printed in the papers. For instance, she said she could see what the boy was wearing.

Police Officer Donald Vicaro was *intrigued*. He asked Allison what else she could "see". Allison told him that the boy's shoes were on the wrong feet. She said she saw a number "8" and a school with a *fence* around it. She also saw a gray house and a factory.

A few weeks later, the boy's body was finally found. It had been

---

孩在当地的一条河里溺水而死，不过他是在多萝西·阿里森做的那个梦两个小时之后才掉进河里的。

当阿里森报警的时候，警方仍在寻找小男孩的尸体。他们可不想被胡乱做梦的家庭妇女打扰。报纸报道了这个案件。所以，警方以为阿里森是读报得到的消息。可是多萝西·阿里森还知道一些报纸没有刊登的情况。比方说，她说她能看到那个小男孩穿什么衣服。

唐纳·维卡罗警官很好奇，便问她还能"看"到些什么。阿里森告诉他说男孩的鞋穿反了。她说她看到一个数字"8"和一个被栅栏包围的学校，也看到一幢灰色的房子和一个工厂。

几周后，男孩的尸体最终被找到了，尸体被顺流冲到附近的池塘里。

---

housewife *n.* 家庭主妇　　　　　　intrigue *v.* 激起……的兴趣
fence *n.* 栅栏

washed downstream into a nearby *pond*. When Officer Vicaro arrived at the scene, he could hardly believe his eyes. There, next to the pond, was Public School Number 8. Around the school was a fence. A factory stood in the distance and so did a gray house. Vicaro checked the boy's body. As Dorothy Allison had predicted, the shoes were on the wrong feet!

Dorothy Allison is a *psychic*. She seems to have special powers to "see" things. Some of her visions come from faraway places. Some come from the future; others come from the past. Allison is not sure how or why she has these visions. She only knows that she's been getting them since childhood.

After the case of the boy who had drowned, police asked Allison

---

当维卡罗警官到达现场时，几乎不能相信他自己的眼睛。在那池塘边就是公立第八中学，学校周围就是栅栏，远处还耸立着一座工厂和一栋灰房子。维卡罗检查了男孩的尸体，正像多萝西·阿里森说得那样，鞋子反穿着。

多萝西·阿里森是个灵异人士。她似乎有特殊的力量，可以"看"到更多的东西。她的幻想有的来自遥远的地方，有的来自未来，有的来自过去。阿里森也不知道她怎么会有这些幻象。她只知道从小时候起，就如此了。

在男孩溺水案之后，警方请阿里森帮助侦破一些其他的案子。到

---

pond *n.* 池塘   psychic *n.* 灵媒

to help solve other crimes. By 1987, she had helped crack hundreds of cases. She does not take any pay for her work. She is just happy when her visions can be put to good use. Often Allison herself does not know what her visions mean. As one detective says, "she may see things backwards, forwards, in the middle....It's up to the police to put the information in some kind of order." Adds one *sheriff*, "Working with a psychic is like doing a crossword puzzle!"

Allison is not the only psychic who has helped solve crimes. There are hundreds like her. In Delavan, Illinois, police sometimes turn to Greta Alexander. In 1977 Alexander told police where to find two drowned *victims*. Six years later, she helped out again. A woman had been missing for a month. Alexander told police to go to a wooded spot near the town of Peoria. There, she said, the woman's body would be found near a bridge. A pile of rocks or salt would also

---

1987年为止，她已经侦破了几百起案件。她分文不取，只是为自己的幻象能对社会有帮助而感到高兴。阿里森经常都不明白自己的幻象是什么意思。就像一个侦探所讲，"她能看到过去的事，将来的事，现在的事。但要靠警方把这些信息梳理排序。"一位警长补充说："和一位灵异人士共事就像玩字谜。"

阿里森并不是唯一一位帮助警方破案的灵士。还有成百上千像她一样的人。在伊利诺伊州的德拉文。警方就经常去求助于格里塔·亚历山大。1977年，亚历山大指引警方到那里去找两个溺水而死的受害者。6年后，她又再次帮忙，一位女士已经走失一个月了。亚历山大告诉警方去佩粤里亚城附近一处植满树木的地方。她说，这位妇女的尸体会在一座桥附近找到，也会有一堆岩石或盐。她告诫警方说，那女士的头与身体是分开的，

---

sheriff *n.* 州长；郡治安官   victim *n.* 受害者

be found there. She warned police that the woman's head would be *detached* from her body. Alexander was right on all counts.

Pennsylvania psychic Nancy Czetli has worked on more than a hundred cases. She has helped solve murders. She has helped find *kidnappers* and track down *burglars*. In January of 1988, she was asked to find a 78-year-old man who had gone out for a walk but never returned. Police had searched for him for a week. They had used dogs, a helicopter—everything. They had found no trace of him. Yet when Czetli looked at an old photograph of the man, she could sense right away what had happened. He had died from the cold. Czetli pointed out the path he had followed. She led police right to the spot where his body was found.

Texas psychic John Catchings began working with police in 1980.

亚历山大的幻象全部得到了证实。

宾夕法尼亚州的灵士南茜·克泽特里已经破了一百多个案子。她曾帮助侦破谋杀案，帮助找到绑匪和窃贼。1988年1月，她被请去帮助寻找一位出门散步就一直未归的78岁的老先生。警方已经查了一周，他们派出了警犬，甚至直升机——用了一切办法，但却一无所获。然而当克泽特里看到老人的一张旧照片时，她立刻感觉出所发生的事。他是死于寒冷。克泽特里指出了他死前的路线，领警察们找到了老人死尸的所在的地方。

得克萨斯州的灵士约翰·卡亭斯是在1980年开始与警方合作的。他

---

detach *v.* 分离
burglar *n.* 窃贼

kidnapper *n.* 绑匪

He was asked to help find an 18-year-old boy who had disappeared. Catchings felt at once that the boy had been murdered. He asked to hold something that had belonged to the boy. He was given the boy's high school ring. "When I held the ring," Catchings says, "I saw a white house with peeling paint, a *trail* behind the house, weeds, an old tire, a shoe, a *creek*."

Police recognized the place Catchings described. It was near the missing boy's home. Catchings announced that the boy's body would be found there. "An old shoe will be the marker," he said. "You'll find the boy's left heel and ankle exposed."

Police had already searched the property once. But they decided to look again. Sure enough, this time they noticed a tree with tires *piled up* around it. On top of one tire was a *sandal*. Could that be the

---

被请去帮忙寻找一位失踪的18岁男孩。卡亭斯立刻便感觉到男孩是被谋杀了。他要求拿一件属于男孩的东西。有人把男孩高中的指环给了他。卡亭斯说，"当我手里拿着这枚指环时，我看到了一座掉了漆的白房子。房后的小径，还有杂草，一个旧轮胎，一只鞋和一条小溪。"

警方认出了卡亭斯所描述的地方。那离男孩的家不远。卡亭斯声称男孩的尸体就会在那找到。他说："一只旧鞋就是标志，你会发现男孩的左脚后跟和脚踝是裸露着的。"

其实警方已经搜查过了那个地方，但他们还是决定再查一遍。这次，他们注意了一棵周围轮胎堆得很高的大树，在轮胎的顶端挂着一只拖鞋。难道这就是卡亭斯提到的那只鞋吗？当警察搬开这些轮胎时，他们看到一

---

trail *n.* 小径

pile up 堆放起来

creek *n.* 小溪

sandal *n.* 凉鞋；拖鞋

shoe Catchings mentioned? When police moved the tires, they saw a heel sticking out of the ground. *Digging up* the dirt, they found the body of the missing boy.

Psychics work in a variety of ways. Some "see" crimes in their dreams. Some say they can read the mind of a victim. Even after a person has died, they say, his or her thought patterns linger on in the brain. By reading those patterns, they can find out what happened. "I don't become the victim," says Nancy Czetli, "but it's as if I'm standing alongside him."

Many psychics also use *psychometry*. This involves getting information from objects. Psychics may ask to hold something

---

只伸出地面的脚跟。挖开泥土，发现这里正埋着失踪男孩的尸首。

灵士们在很多方面起作用。有一些说在梦中"看到"罪犯，另一些说他们可以解读受害者的心理。他们说，甚至在一个人死后，他们的思维方式仍在大脑中徘徊。通过对这些思维模式的解读，他们可以分析出很多发生过的事。南茜·克泽特里说，"我并不会变成受害者本身，但就像我和他站在一起一样。"

很多灵士也会运用心灵占卜术。这包括从一些物体上获取信息。灵士

---

dig up 挖出

psychometry *n.* 心理测验

that belonged to the victim. It could be anything. It could be an old hat or—as in John Catchings's famous case—a high school ring. Psychics say they can get vibrations from these things. By feeling the *vibrations*, they can tell what happened to the object's owner.

Psychics have not convinced everyone. Some people still scoff at them. Dr. Martin Reiser has done studies for the Los Angeles Police Department. He says psychics are of no use to police. But more and more people are *echoing* the words of Detective Ron Phillips. "I felt it was baloney at first," he said. But then Phillips worked with John Catchings. "He made me believe [in psychics]," Phillips said. "They've got a power there—it gives you goose bumps, really."

们会要求手拿一些属于受害者的东西，什么都可以。可以是个旧帽子，或者就像约翰·卡亭斯的著名案件中那样，是一枚高中的指环。灵士们说他们可从这些东西上接收到感应。通过这些感应，他们便可知这些东西的主人都发生了什么事情。

灵士们并没有让每个人都相信。一些人仍对其抱以嘲笑。马丁·雷瑟医生曾为洛杉矶警局作研究。他说灵士对警方毫无用处。但越来越多的人附和着唐·飞利浦侦探的话。他说："我开始也感觉那纯粹是一派胡言，"但他当时正和约翰·卡亭斯一起共事。飞利浦说："他让我相信灵士，他们的确有股力量——真的让你大吃一惊。"

---

vibration n. 心灵感应   echo v. 呼应

Mummies

Have you ever thought of being a *mummy* for Halloween? You could probably do it just by wrapping yourself in a bunch of white *bandages*. But making a real mummy is not so easy. First, you need a dead body. And second, you need someone who understands the ancient art of mummy making.

The people of ancient Egypt believed that spirits of the dead still needed their bodies in the afterlife. So after people died, their bodies were given special treatment to keep them from decaying. Bodies undergoing this complicated treatment are called mummies.

木乃伊

古代的埃及人相信死人的灵魂在后世仍需要肉身。所以人们在死后，他们的身体会经过特殊的处理以防腐烂。经过这些繁杂处理的身体被称为木乃伊。

你曾想过万圣节时扮成一具木乃伊吗？你可能仅是把自己缠在一堆白色绷带里。但制作一个真正的木乃伊，可不只这样简单。首先，要有一具死尸。其次，还要有人懂得古老的木乃伊制作技术。

mummy *n.* 木乃伊   bandage *n.* 绷带

A mummy is not the same as a *skeleton*. A skeleton is just bones. But a mummy has bones and skin. Often it has hair, fingernails, and muscles as well. Usually, these softer body parts decay quickly. But that does not happen with mummies. If a mummy has been properly prepared, it can last a long, long time.

Ancient Egyptians were master mummy makers. Some of their mummies are now more than three thousand years old. These bodies still have lips, noses, and ears. They have eyelids and *toenails*. One has red hair. Another has a face twisted in a scream of death made thousands of years ago.

How did the Egyptians make such great mummies? Their secret was to dry each body thoroughly. If a body is totally dry, the flesh won't rot away. Drying a body means getting rid of all the *fluids* in it. To do this, Egyptians slit open the side of each body. They *scooped*

一个木乃伊和一架骷髅是不一样的。后者仅是骨头，而前者有骨还有皮，还经常会有头发、指甲和肌肉。通常来讲，这些较软的部分很快就会腐烂掉。然而木乃伊却并不如此。如果制作得好的话，就可以保存很长的时间。

古代的埃及人是制造木乃伊的大师。他们的一些木乃伊至今已经有了三千多年的历史。这些尸体仍有嘴唇、鼻子、耳朵，有眼皮，有脚趾甲。其中一具有红色的头发，另一个几千年以前所制的，脸部因死亡的尖叫而变形。

那么埃及人是如何制作出如此精良的木乃伊呢？他们的秘密就是将尸体彻底干燥。如果一具尸体完全干燥的话，肉体便不会腐烂。干燥一具尸体意思是将其中的所有水分都除去。这样，埃及人从侧面割开每具尸体，

---

skeleton n. 骨架
fluid n. 液体

toenail n. 脚趾甲
scoop v. 挖出

out much of the insides. They took out the stomach. They took out the liver, *intestines*, and *lungs*. They did not take out the heart, however. They believed the heart was the center of wisdom and truth. So they left that alone.

The brain was removed through the nose. Mummy makers stuck a long metal hook up the nose of the body. They scrambled the brain and partially liquefied it. Then they stored it and other organs in jars.

Once Egyptians had cleaned out a body, they washed it with wine. They packed it with a special salt called *natron*. Then they sat back and waited for 40 days. During that time, the natron soaked up liquid from the body. By the end of the 40 days, no liquid was left.

The drying-out process left bodies as shriveled as *prunes*. But Egyptians solved that problem too. They stuffed the bodies with cloth or sand. That puffed the skin back up again. Sometimes they

---

挖出绝大部分内脏。他们掏出胃、肝脏、肠子和肺，却并不挖出心脏。他们认为心脏是智慧和真理的中心。所以，他们唯独把心脏留在原位。

大脑是通过鼻子取出的。木乃伊制作者把一个长金属钩伸入尸体的鼻子里。他们搅碎尸体的大脑，把它部分液化。取出后，他们将其和其他器官存放在罐子里。

一旦埃及人把一个尸体收拾干净后，便会用酒清洗，再塞满一种特殊的盐，叫作天然碳酸钠，然后放置40天。在这段时间里，这种盐碱会吸干尸体里的水分。40天后，尸体里就不会再有液体了。

整个干燥的过程让尸体就像李子干一样褶皱。埃及人同样也解决了这个问题。他们把尸体塞满布或沙土。那让尸体的皮肤又松胀起来。有时

---

intestine *n.* 肠

natron *n.* 天然碳酸钠

lung *n.* 肺

prune *n.* 李子干

put *peppercorns* up the nose. That helped push the nose back to its original shape. Egyptians also rubbed spices and herbs on the body to mask the smell of death.

Next, mummy makers coated the dried body with a glue called resin. As the resin dried, it became hard. It formed a tough coating that protected the body. It made the body waterproof.

Finally, Egyptians wrapped each body in 20 layers of cloth. This was a *tricky* task. It took many days and required about 150 yards of cloth. Sometimes an ear or toe fell off during the wrapping. But by the time the last layer was put on, the mummy was close to normal size again.

From 2600 B.C. to A.D. 300, Egyptians made millions of mummies. Almost everyone in Egypt who could afford it became one. Egyptians also mummified animals. They made cat mummies

---

候，他们把胡椒粒塞进鼻孔，这样可以帮助把鼻子恢复成原来的形状。埃及人也把香料和药草涂擦在尸体上以掩盖死尸的气味。

然后，他们把已经干燥完毕的尸体表面涂上一层名为松脂的胶。松胶干后就变硬，会变成一个结实的表层保护尸体，可以防水。

最后，埃及人再把每个尸体都包上20层布。这是一项复杂而棘手的工作。要花上好多天，用上150码布。有时，在包裹过程中，耳朵或脚趾都会掉下来。但等到最后一层布被包上去的时候，木乃伊的大小就和身体差不多了。

从公元前2600年到公元300年间，埃及人制作了数百万的木乃伊。几乎每一个负担得起费用的埃及人在死后都被制成木乃伊，埃及人也做动物的木

---

peppercorn *n.* 干胡椒   tricky *adj.* 复杂的

and dog mummies. They turned fish, snakes, and birds into mummies. They even made mummies out of *grasshoppers* and *beetles*!

There was a reason for this "mummy mania." Egyptians thought living things needed their bodies after death. They believed dead people went on to the land of the gods. Even dead animals moved on to an "afterlife." Spirits of the dead could make contact with the gods. But those spirits still needed a place to rest at night. They needed to return to their bodies. If their bodies had *rotted away*, the spirits would have no place to rest. Then the spirits, too, would die.

Ancient Egyptians were not the only ones who believed in life after death. And they were not the only ones who made mummies. Halfway across the world, in the mountains of South America, people did the same thing. By 3000 B.C., people in Peru and Chile

---

乃伊，他们做猫的，狗的，也把鱼、蛇和鸟做成木乃伊，甚至蚱蜢和甲虫。

这样的木乃伊狂热症是不无原因的。埃及人认为生物在死后仍需要身体。他们相信人死后会继续踏向神灵的土地。甚至动物死后也会继续它们的"后世"。死者的灵魂会和神灵沟通，但这些灵魂在夜间仍然需要一个地方休息，它们需要回到自己身体里面去。如果身体腐烂了，灵魂无处安歇，灵魂便也会死掉。

古代的埃及人并不是唯一相信后世的人群。也并不是只有他们制作木乃伊。绕过半个地球，在南美洲的大山里人们做着同样的事情。公元前3000年，秘鲁和智利的人们就已经掌握如何保存死尸了。他们并不用

---

grasshopper *n.* 蚱蜢   beetle *n.* 甲虫
rot away 烂掉

had figured out how to preserve dead bodies. They did not dry them with salt. Instead, they set them out in the hot sun. Sometimes they also put them over a fire. The heat and smoke helped to get rid of all liquids. Once the bodies were dry, they were wrapped up and put in baskets. In Egypt, mummies were stretched out flat. But most South American mummies had their knees folded up to their *chins*.

Mummies are not always thousands of years old. About 400 years ago, some people in Italy started making mummies. They felt it would help them keep in touch with the spirits of those who had died. These Italians put the bodies in a special room. They left them there for a year. During that time, all fluids drained out of the bodies. Then the bodies were laid in the sun. When they were fully dried, they were dressed in fancy clothes. They were put in underground rooms called *catacombs*.

盐来干燥，而是把尸体放在灼热的太阳下暴晒。有时候，也放到火上烘。热量和烟能帮助除去水分。一旦尸体干燥后便会包起来放在篮子里。在埃及，木乃伊被平放。而在南美，大多数木乃伊的膝盖被对折到下巴处。

木乃伊并不总有几千年的历史。大约在四百年前，一些意大利人开始制作木乃伊。他们认为这样会帮他们和死者的灵魂保持联系。这些意大利人把尸体放在一间特殊的房间里，在那放一年。在那段时间里，水分会被排出体外。然后，这些尸体会被晾放在太阳下晒，当彻底被晒干后，会被穿上漂亮的衣服，然后被放到叫作地下墓穴的地下室里。

---

chin *n.* 下巴　　　　　　　　　　　catacomb *n.* 地下墓穴

People often visited the mummies in the catacombs. They brought picnic lunches to eat. They talked to the mummies, asking them for advice. Some people even held hands with the mummies as they said prayers.

The last Italian mummy was created in 1920. It was made from the body of a little girl named Rosali Lombardo. Rosali died at the age of two. Her father was a doctor. He knew how to mummify dead bodies. In fact, he had developed a new system for it. Dr. Lombardo used his system on little Rosali. The results were amazing. Rosali's body is perfectly preserved. It has not *shriveled* at all. In fact, it looks as though Rosali is just taking a *nap*. No one knows what Dr. Lombardo's system was. He died before sharing it with the world.

Some people think mummies are a good way to honor the dead. But others don't even like to look at them. You might want to keep that in mind if you ever do dress up like a mummy for Halloween.

　　人们会时常去地下墓穴看这些木乃伊。他们会带午餐去那吃，会和木乃伊说话，询问意见。一些人甚至在祈祷时和木乃伊握手。

　　一具意大利木乃伊在1920年制成，是用一个名为罗萨里·伦巴多的小女孩的身体制成的。罗萨里在两岁的时候就死了。她的父亲是个医生，知道如何制作木乃伊。实际上，他发明了一种新的方法。伦巴多医生把这种方法用在小罗萨里身上，结果是惊人的。罗萨里的身体被保存的完好无缺，丝毫没有褶皱。实际上，就像罗萨里在打瞌睡一样。没人知道伦巴多医生的方法是怎样的，在公之于众前他就去世了。

　　一些人认为木乃伊是向死者致敬的好方法，但有些人连看一眼都不愿意。如果你曾经在万圣节上扮成木乃伊的话，你很可能情愿只把那记在脑子里而已。

---

shrivel *v.* 皱缩

nap *n.* 小睡

12

Near-Death Experiences

At 1:38 on a Tuesday afternoon, Richard Selzer died. He had lain in a *coma* for 23 days, and, finally, his heart stopped beating. The doctor and nurses did all they could to get it going again. They gave Selzer electric shocks. They injected medicine right into his *chest*. But at 1:38 P.M. on April 23, 1991, the doctor declared, "This

Imagine that you have been seriously injured in a car crash. You stop breathing and then rise above your body. Free of pain, you float through a tunnel toward a bright light. But the light fades and you hear someone yell, "This victim is breathing again!" You are one of the millions who have had a Near–Death Experience.

死里逃生

　　想象一下你在一场车祸中严重受伤。你停止了呼吸，然后飞离了你的身体。没有了病痛，你通过一个隧道飘向一缕亮光。但这光消逝了，你听到有人叫道："这个人又有呼吸了！"那么，你就和几百万人一样体验了一场死里逃生的经历。

　　在周二下午1:38，理查德·赛尔泽死了。他已经昏迷了23天，最终心脏停止了跳动。医生和护士做了一切努力让它重新跳动起来。他们给赛尔泽进行了电击，直接向胸口注射了药物，可在1991年4月23日下午1:38，医生还是宣布："他死了。"，而当10分钟后，理查德·赛尔泽又开始呼

---

coma *n.* 昏迷　　　　　　　　　　　　　　　　chest *n.* 胸

man is dead." Imagine everyone's surprise when, 10 minutes later, Richard Selzer began breathing again.

No one knows just how Selzer did it. During the minutes he was "dead", he had no *heartbeat*. He drew no breath. Yet he can describe what went on in the hospital room during those minutes. In 1993 he laid it all out in a book titled *Raising the Dead*.

In the book, Selzer details the feeling of being outside his body. Looking down at the hospital bed from above, he could see what was happening. He saw the movements made by nurses after he was declared dead. Just before coming back to life, he heard the beating of *wings*. Then he felt a veil lifting from his face. That was when he began to breathe again.

Richard Selzer is not the only one who has had this kind of brush

---

吸时，可想而知，所有人是何等惊诧。

没人知道赛尔泽是如何做到的，在他"死去"的那几分钟里，他没有了心跳，也停止了呼吸，然而却可以描述出那几分钟里医院所发生的事情。1993年，他在《起死回生》这本书中完整地描述了他的那段经历。

在书中，赛尔泽详细地描述了他灵魂出窍的感觉。从上空往下俯视医院的病床，他可以看到正在发生的一切。他可以看到在他被宣布已死亡之后，护士们的动作。就在重返生命之前，他听到翅膀的震颤声。然后感到一块面纱从他脸上揭起，从那时起他又开始了呼吸。

理查德·赛尔泽并不是唯一有这种与死亡擦肩而过的经历的人。在

---

heartbeat *n.* 心跳　　　　　　　　　　　　　　　　　wing *n.* 翅膀

with death. In a 1982 poll, 8 million Americans reported that they had had Near-Death Experiences, or NDEs. One woman had one when her heart stopped during *surgery*. Another had one after a bad motorcycle crash. A boy had one when he fell into a *washtub* and almost drowned.

What happens to people during the time they are "dead"? Different people report different things. Still, patterns have formed. Like Richard Selzer, many say they leave their bodies. One person who returned from near death put it this way: "I was out of my body and out of pain. I was up on the *ceiling* in a corner of the room, looking down, watching doctors and nurses rush around frantically as they worked to save my life." Another said, "I remember just floating up through darkness." Writes David Wheeler, "I felt myself

---

1982年的一场调查中，有800万美国人宣称自己曾有过这种经历，简称NDE（near-death experience）。一位女士在手术过程中曾有过一次这种经历。另一个人在一场可怕的摩托车撞毁事件后也经历过。一个男孩在掉进大洗衣盆里几乎溺水时也经历了一次。

在人们"死亡"的时候，发生些什么？不同的人声称发生不同的事情。但仍然形成了几个模式。像理查德·赛尔泽一样，很多人说他们离开了自己的身体。一个人这样说："我离开了我的身体，没有了病痛。在屋顶上空的一个角落里俯视，看着医生和护士们在抢救我时忙乱地跑来跑去。"另一个人说："我就记得我在黑暗中向上飘浮。"大卫·韦勒写

---

surgery *n.* 外科手术　　　　　　　　　washtub *n.* 洗衣盆
ceiling *n.* 天花板

moving away from my physical body.... I started to float just a little distance above my body."

Next, people often say, they move through a *tunnel*. They travel toward a bright light. Along the way, they may meet dead relatives. Or they may look back over their whole life. For most people, these moments are pleasant. According to David Wheeler, "I was not frightened. It was a good feeling." Others agree. One woman said, "What I saw while I was dead was so beautiful." Another man claimed his NDE "was the most relaxing and joyful experience of my life."

For a few, though, NDEs bring terror. These people feel they are entering a giant *void*. They see nothing but dark, empty space. One woman felt she was "falling into a deep well. The fall never seemed

道："我感到自己从我的肉身那飞离，开始在我身体上空不远的地方飘浮。"

然后，人们常说，他们穿过了一条隧道，飞向一缕亮光。途中，他们还可能会遇到死去的亲属。或者能回顾到自己的一生。对大多数人来讲，这段经历都是美好的。根据大卫·韦勒的说法，"我并不害怕，反而感觉非常好。"其他人也都同意。一位女士说，"我死亡时所见的都如此美妙。"另一个人更声称他的NDE是"他一生中最美好快乐的时光"。

然而，对少数人来讲，NDE却带来了恐惧。这些人感觉他们进入了一个巨大的空虚之所。他们只见到了一片黑暗，空空如也。一位女士感到她

tunnel *n.* 隧道

void *n.* 空虚；空间

to end. I was alone in a strange and unfamiliar world...."

People who have had Near-Death Experiences—good or bad—feel their journeys were somehow interrupted. Some say they were pulled back to their bodies. Others say they were sent back against their will. In either case, their hearts resumed beating and they were once again "alive."

Are people making up these stories? Perhaps. But it's hard to believe that 8 million folks are lying. So what is going on? Do people really leave their bodies during NDEs? Some scientists say no. They say people may think they are floating. But that feeling is caused by lack of oxygen to the brain. Dr. Bruce Greyson disagrees. Grey son is a college professor. He has spent 20 years studying NDEs. He points out that lack of oxygen causes *confusion* and *panic*. NDEs, on

---

"坠入了一口极深的井。那一跌似乎永无休止，感觉自己在一个奇怪而陌生的世界里……"

有过NDE经历的人们——无论好坏——都感觉他们被打断了。一些人说他们是被拽回到身体里的。另一些人说他们不情愿地被送回去。但两种情况下都一样，他们的心脏恢复了跳动，又"活"了过来。

难道是人们编出了这些故事吗？或许如此，但要相信800万人都在说谎实在太难了。那么到底是怎么回事？莫非在NDE过程中人们真的离开了身体？一些科学家说并不是那样。他们说人们可能以为自己在飘浮，但那种感觉是由于大脑缺氧而引起的。布鲁斯·格雷森医生却并不赞同。格雷森医生是位大学教授，已经进行了20年的NDE研究，他指出缺氧会导致迷

---

confusion *n.* 混乱　　　　　　　　panic *n.* 恐慌

the other hand, bring calm, clear thoughts.

Could NDEs simply be dreams? Greyson throws out that theory too. Dreams, he says, don't change people's lives. Near-Death Experiences do. NDEs leave people happier and less fearful. After NDEs, people tend to focus on helping others. They may give up high-paying jobs to do work that pays less but is more satisfying.

Dr. Sherwin Nuland is not convinced. He thinks NDEs are caused by chemicals in the brain. He says these chemicals are *sent out* in times of shock. But Nuland can't explain all parts of NDEs. Sometimes, for instance, people pick up information while they float outside their bodies. Greyson tells of a woman who "died" for a short time. While doctors worked to bring her back, Greyson talked with the woman's roommate. Later, the woman could describe that whole

---

惑不安和恐慌，而NDE却只会带来平静，清晰的想象。

NDE可能仅仅是梦而已吗？格雷森医生也排除了这个理论。他说，梦并不会改变人的生活，可NDE会，它让人们多了快乐而少了不安。在经历了NDE之后，人们总是大多数乐于助人。他们可能会放弃高收入的职业而去做一些收入少却更令人有满足感的工作。

谢文·努力兰德并不相信这种解释。他认为NDE是由大脑中的某些化学物质引起的。他说这些化学物在人们受惊之时产生。但努力兰德并不能完全地解释NDE。比如，有时当人们在身体之外飘浮时，他们也会得到信息。格雷森医生讲述了一个"死"了一小会的女士。当医生抢救她时，格雷森医生正和她的一个室友谈话。而后来，这位女士却可以描述出那次谈

---

send out 放出；发送

conversation. Said Greyson, "Even if she had been conscious, she couldn't possibly have overheard. We were too far away."

Sooner or later, we will all find out for ourselves what happens when we die. But people who have had NDEs urge us not to rush things. They enjoyed their contact with death. But they still want to continue their lives here on earth. As Dr. Greyson notes, an NDE does not make someone *suicidal*. "On the contrary," he says, "it makes life more attractive."

话的内容。他说："即使她当时是有意识和知觉的。也不太可能听到，我们离她太远了。"

　　总有一天，当我们自己死的时候，会发现究竟将发生什么。但经历过NDE的人们让我们不要着急。他们很乐意享受与死亡的接触。但他们仍然想继续在人世生活。正像格雷森医生所说的那样，NDE并不会让谁自杀，他说："正相反，这反而会让生活更有魅力。"

---

suicidal *adj.* 自杀的

13

Is Anyone Out There?

Is there *intelligent* life elsewhere in the universe? Some people would answer that question with a loud "Yes!" In fact, some people would say that space travelers from other worlds visit us all the time. As proof, these people would point to UFOs (Unidentified Flying Objects). There are thousands of UFO sightings every

Even the Hubble Space Telescope shown here cannot focus on anything so small as a planet around a distant star. Still, many scientists believe that there are many planets in the universe that can support life. Will creatures from those planets ever contact us? Are they trying to contact us now?

太空生物

即使哈勃太空望远镜也无法观察像一颗遥远的恒星周围的行星那么小的物体。但仍有很多科学家相信宇宙中的很多星球都可以支持生命体。那么那些星球的生物曾经和我们联系吗？还是正在尽力和我们联系？

在宇宙的其他地方还有高等生物吗？一些人会极为肯定地回答道"是"。事实上，一些人会说我们一直都有来自其他世界的宇宙来访者。这些人会拿UFO（不明飞行物）作为证据，每年都有成千上万的UFO目击

intelligent *adj.* 智能的

year. Believers say UFOs are really spaceships from other *planets*. So for UFO fans, there is no question. They are sure someone else is "out there" and, in fact, is watching us all the time.

Yet despite all the sightings, most scientists do not believe in UFOs. There are a couple of reasons for this. For one thing, how would creatures from some other planet know about us? We have been sending radio signals to outer space for only a few years. These *signals* have not had time to reach any distant planets. Our nearest neighbors may be hundreds of light-years away. (A light-year measures how far light travels in one year. The speed of light is 186,000 miles per second.) So if we do have neighbors, they won't get our radio signals for years to come.

Some people think aliens could have noticed us even without radio signals. If that's the case, they say, couldn't these aliens drop

事件。相信的人都说UFO的确是来自其他星球的飞船。所以，对UFO迷们来讲，这没有什么好疑问的。他们确信地球之外还有生物，而且，事实上，他们也正一直在看着我们。

然而，尽管有这么多的目击事件。大多数科学家并不相信UFO的存在。有这么几个原因。其一，其他某个星球的生物是如何知晓我们的？只是近几年来我们才向太空发射无线电讯号。这些信号还没有来得及抵达哪个较远的星球。离我们最近的邻居可能在几百光年之外。（光年是衡量光在一年里能走多远，而光速是每秒186,000英里。）所以，如果我们真有邻居的话，在未来的几年内，他们是不会收到我们的无线电讯号的。

一些人认为即使没有无线电讯号，外星人也会注意到我们的。如果真是如此的话，他们说，难道这些外星人不会时不时地顺便走访一下我们？

planet *n.* 行星　　　　　　　　　　　　　signal *n.* 信号

by for a visit from time to time? It's not likely. Certainly humans have not figured out a way to whiz from one *solar* system to another. Again, it's a distance problem. The nearest star is more than four light-years away. It would take our best spaceship 100,000 years to get there! And most stars are much, much farther away.

So if aliens were going to visit us, they'd have to be a lot smarter than we are. They would have to figure out how to fly close to the speed of light. Some distant civilization might have the skills to do that. But, again, most scientists doubt it. Besides, suppose that some life form is that advanced. Why would these creatures want to visit Earth? Compared to them, humans would seem pretty simple-minded. So if aliens were going to *zip* off to some other planet, chances are it wouldn't be ours.

这不太可能。当然，人类尚未想出哪个办法可以从一个太阳系到另外一个去。同样是距离的问题。离地球最近的恒星约四光年那么远。即使最好的宇宙飞船也要花100,000年才能到达那里。并且大多数恒星离我们要更远。

所以，如果外星人真要来访的话，他们必须要比我们聪明很多。他们必须知道如何以接近光的速度飞行。一些遥远的文明或许可以具备这样的技能。然而，同样地，大多数科学家对其表示质疑。此外，假设真有某种生物如此高级，那他们又为什么想走访地球呢？与他们相比，人类会显得头脑过于简单，所以，如果外星人要尖啸而驰到另一个星球上去，很可能不会是我们的地球。

---

solar *adj.* 太阳的   zip *v.* 以尖啸声行进；使沿某方向快速移动

Given all this, it seems safe to conclude that UFOs are not for real. Little green people in flying saucers are probably not flashing through the sky every year to check us out. Does that mean that there is no intelligent life anywhere else in the universe? Not at all! Most scientists believe there is lots of intelligent life out there. Just look at the facts. In our *galaxy* alone—the Milky Way—there are about 400 billion stars. There is a strong chance that many of these stars have planets that can support life. Scientists have made a *rough* guess about how many. They figure that there may be as many as 10,000 civilizations in the Milky Way. Now consider that there are at least 400 billion galaxies! Surely these other galaxies also contain planets that could support life.

鉴于这些，似乎断定有UFO并不是真的具有多少可信度。飞碟里的绿色小人不太可能每年都闪过天空来拜访我们。难道那就意味着宇宙的其他角落都没有智能生命了吗？并不然。大多数科学家都认为外空里有很多的高等生物。看看这个事实。单单我们的星系——银河系——就有4000亿颗恒星。很可能其中有许多恒星里可以支持生命的存在。科学家们大约地推测了一下，推算出在银河系里可能有10,000个文明世界。现在，来想一下至少4000亿个星系吧！当然其他星系里也会有包含能够支撑生命体的行星。

---

galaxy *n.* 银河   rough *adj.* 粗略的

It's frustrating to think that we might never see the life forms that inhabit other planets. But couldn't we at least talk to them? Scientists say that is possible. It could be done using radio *waves*. These waves travel at the speed of light. Even here, though, there are some problems. Imagine radio signals coming from a planet that is 10,000 light-years away. By the time we get these signals, the creatures who sent them might no longer exist. After all, it would have taken the signals 10,000 years to reach Earth. A lot can happen in that time. Think about our own civilization. Will the human race be here 10,000 years from now? Or will some disease have killed us all? Will we have *wiped* ourselves out with wars or pollution? No one knows the answer. In fact, there are no guarantees we'll last even another hundred years. So by the time creatures on another planet

---

　　想到我们或许永远都不会有机会看到栖息于其他星球的生命体。的确有些令人沮丧。但是，难道我们至少连和他们说话都不行吗？科学家们说是可能的，可以通过无线电波来实现。这些电波以光速移动。即使如此，还是存在着一些问题，想象一下无线电波从10,000光年之遥的星球而来。到我们接收到这些信号时，发射它们的生物可能已经不复存在了。毕竟，这信号要抵达地球要花上10,000年。那期间，很多事情都能发生——想一下我们的文明世界。10,000年之后，人类还会存在吗？或者某种疾病会让我们人类灭绝吗？我们会以战争和污染自我毁灭吗？没人知道答案。事实上，没人能担保人类会再生存100年。所以等到另一个星球的生物接收到我们的无线电讯号时，我们可能已经不在好久了。

---

wave *n.* 波动　　　　　　　　　　　　　　wipe *v.* 消除

receive our radio signals, we might be long gone.

There's one more thing to keep in mind. The life that exists on another planet might not look anything at all like human life. Scientists urge us to stop thinking in terms of "little green men." In truth, we have no idea what other forms of intelligent life would look like. Like us, they would most likely be made up of *atoms* and *molecules*. But beyond that, it's anyone's guess. They could be as different from us as we are from *alligators*. Also, the idea of flying saucers is ours, not theirs. If aliens did visit us, their technology would be far beyond ours. It would be beyond anything we could imagine. As scientist Carl Sagan has said, it would look to us as if the creatures were performing "magic."

　　还有一件事要铭记在心。另一个星球的生命体很可能看起来与我们人类相当不同。科学家们让我们不要再想"绿色小人"之类的事情。事实上，我们并不了解其他形式的高级生命体会长成什么样子。像我们一样，他们最可能由原子和分子构成。但除此之外，便纯是个人猜测了。他们可能与我们非常不同，就像我们与鳄鱼不同一样。同样，有关飞碟的想法是我们的，而并不是他们的。如果，外星人真的拜访我们的话，他们的科技会超出我们所想。正如科学家卡尔·芹根所言，"在我们看来，那会像外星人在施魔法一样。"

---

atom *n.* 原子　　　　　　　　　　　　　　　　molecule *n.* 分子
alligator *n.* 短吻鳄

WEIRD SCIENCE

It's All in Your Head

"You are what you eat."
Have you ever been told
that as you pop potato chips into
your mouth? Actually, it's a pretty
fair warning. Your body turns the
food you eat into blood, bones, and
muscles. Eat bad food and you will
probably *end up with* a weak body. Eat
good food and you will probably end
up with a strong body.

Through modern technology, researchers can attach special wires to patients' skin to find out what's happening inside. The wires pick up data about patients' involuntary actions, such as heartbeat and nerve impulses. Then, using the information, patients learn how to control some of these actions.

生物回馈

通过现代科学技术，科研人员可以把特殊的线连到病人的皮肤上去探测身体内部在发生些什么变化。这些线搜集病人无意动作的信息，比如心跳和神经脉搏。而后，病人可以运用这些信息去学会如何控制自己的一些无意动作。

"吃什么，你就是什么。"在把薯片丢进嘴里的时候，是否有人曾告诉过你这个呢？实际上，那是非常正确的告诫。你的身体把你所吃的食物化为血液，筋骨和肌肉。吃的食物不好可能会导致身体虚弱，相反好的食物会使人体魄强健。

fair *adj.* 公平的   end up with 以……而告终

Everyone agrees that eating healthy foods will help make a healthy body. But now scientists are also discovering that "you are what you think." That doesn't mean you can think your way into the Olympics. And it doesn't mean that you can close your eyes and heal a broken leg. But your thoughts, or brain waves, can do some remarkable things. They can cure headaches. They can help lower blood pressure. Your thoughts can even direct messages to certain nerve *cells* in your body. This ability can restore the use of muscles lost through an accident or disease.

This new form of mind control is called *biofeedback*. In truth, it isn't really new. People in Asia have been using biofeedback for centuries. In the United States, however, use of biofeedback is new. It began during the 1960s. Some young people began studying the *religions* of Asia. They learned about biofeedback and began to practice it.

人人都同意健康的饮食对身体的健康会有帮助。但现在科学家们又发现"想什么你就是什么。"那可绝不意味着你一想就可以参加奥运会，也不意味着一闭眼你就可以治愈一条受伤的腿。但是你的思维或者说脑电波的确可以做一些非凡的事情。它们可以治愈头痛，帮助降低血压。你的思维甚至可以把讯息导入你体内的某些神经细胞那去。这种能力使在事故或疾病中丧失功能的肌肉痊愈。

这种新形式的思维控制被称为"生物回馈"。事实上，它并不是新生事物，亚洲人已经运用了几个世纪。然而，在美国，对"生物回馈"的运用的确才刚刚开始没多久。这是在20世纪60年代才开始的。一些年轻人开始研究亚洲的宗教信仰。他们了解了"生物回馈"，并开始实践。这些

---

cell *n.* 细胞   biofeedback *n.* 生物反馈
religion *n.* 宗教

These people used it to help them *meditate*, or focus their thinking. At first, western scientists laughed at biofeedback. They thought it was just a fad. Slowly, however, the practice took hold. One study after another showed that it really worked. Maybe, scientists thought, biofeedback wasn't so crazy after all.

Clearly, your brain can control certain things. For example, it can command your legs to run. It can direct your hand to write a letter. And it can tell your mouth to speak. Those are called voluntary actions. You make up your mind to do something. But your body does other things that are very hard to control. How, for instance, can you control your heartbeat? Or the *circulation* of your blood? Or your body's temperature? Those bodily functions are called involuntary. They just happen. You have no control over them ...

人用"生物回馈"来帮助调解或集中他们的思考。起先，西方的科学家对"生物回馈"嗤以嘲讽，以为那仅是一股风潮而已。然而渐渐地，"生物回馈"站住了脚，一个又一个的研究证实了它的确奏效。也许，科学家们也认为并不是那样疯狂。

很明显，大脑可以控制某些事情。例如，它可以命令你的腿去跑，可以让你的手写信，而且还可以让你的嘴讲话。这些都叫作"有意"动作。你决定去做某件事，但你的身体却做另一些难以控制的事情。例如，你如何才能控制你的心跳？或者血液循环？或者体温？这些身体功能被称为

---

meditate *v.* 考虑   circulation *n.* 循环

or do you? The goal of biofeedback is to help you control those involuntary actions.

Here is how it works. You sit in a chair in front of a TV *monitor*. Special wires are taped to your head, neck, back, and fingers. The wires can detect tiny changes in your body's involuntary actions. The other ends of the wires are *hooked up to* a biofeedback machine. Let's say that you are trying to reduce your heart rate. Soft music begins to play. You try to relax. You might try deep breathing, or you might concentrate on thinking pleasant thoughts. You might imagine yourself lying on the beach in the warm sun. The machine measures your heart rate and "feeds back" information about how well you are doing.

You can see your progress on the TV screen. A line or a series of

"无意"动作。它们就那样发生着，并不受你所控……还是你可以控制？"生物回馈"的目标就是帮助你控制这些无意动作。

它就是这样发生作用的。你在电视屏幕前的一把椅子上坐下。你的头颈后背和手指被粘上特殊的线。这些线可以检查出你身体无意识动作中任何轻微的变化。线的另一端被固定在一台"生物回馈"机上。让我们假设你想要减缓你的心率。柔和的音乐开始奏响，你尽量放松。你可以尝试深呼吸，或者集中心神想美好的事情。想象自己在温暖的阳光下躺在海滩上，"生物回馈"机会测量你的心率。然后，"回馈"有关你的情况的信息。

你可以在电视屏幕上看到自己的进展，一条线或者连续的嘟嘟声记

monitor *n.* 监视器　　　　　　　　hook up to 连接到

beeps records your heart rate. By watching that line, you can learn what thoughts slow down your heart. You might find that an image of a sunny beach lowers your heart rate. But imagining that same beach bathed in *moonlight* does not. Slowly, you learn how to reduce your heart rate. Once this is done, you no longer need the machine. You have learned to control your body's "involuntary" actions.

But biofeedback can work even greater wonders. Since the 1970s, it has been used to help *epileptics* control seizures. These seizures cause epileptics to shake without control. Sometimes they faint. These attacks are caused by electrical discharges in the brain.

Using biofeedback, many epileptics have learned to control their seizures. They discover what feelings or situations trigger seizures.

载你的心率。观察那条线，你会知道想什么会减慢你的心跳。想象一下你在阳光明媚的海滩上，你的心跳会减慢，但沐浴在月光下就会有所不同。慢慢地，你会学会如何减缓自己的心率。一旦学会，便不再需要机器帮助了。你已经学会了如何控制你自身的"无意"动作。

但"生物回馈"却可以有更妙的效果。自从20世纪70年代以来，"生物回馈"一直被用来帮助癫痫病患者控制病情。一旦发作，病人便会无法自控地颤抖，有时还会晕厥。这些都是由大脑电波发射而引起的。

通过运用"生物回馈"，很多癫痫病患者都已经学会了如何控制病情的发作。他们摸索出什么样的情绪或情况会导致病情发作。他们学会避免

moonlight *n.* 月光   epileptic *n.* 癫痫患者

They learn to avoid those feelings. In a sense, then, biofeedback shows epileptics how to "*rewire*" their brains.

Biofeedback can even help badly hurt people. In the 1980s, a car accident left Tammy DeMichael with a broken neck and a crushed *spinal* cord. She had no feeling in her arms or legs. Traditional medicine did nothing to help her. It looked as if she would have to spend the rest of her life in a wheelchair. Luckily, she still had a few good nerves reaching her arm muscles. They were not enough to let DeMichael move her arm, but they gave her some hope.

Could her brain be taught to use those remaining nerves? Bernard Brucker, her doctor, thought so. He hooked DeMichael up to a biofeedback machine. The TV monitor showed a blue line. That line represented impulses moving from her brain through her spine

这些情绪的出现。在某种角度来讲，"生物回馈"让癫痫病患者了解如何给他们的大脑"重新连线"。

"生物回馈"甚至可以帮助重伤人群。早在20世纪80年代，在一场交通事故中，塔米·德马克脖颈受了重伤而且脊柱粉碎性骨折。她的四肢全无知觉，传统的医疗方法对她毫无作用。看起来她只能在轮椅上度过下半生。可幸运的是，她手臂部仍有一些好的神经未损，但它们不足以让德马克挥动手臂。但却给了她希望。

她的大脑可以学会如何运用这些仅存的神经吗？她的医生伯纳德·布鲁克认为可以。他把德马克连在一台"生物回馈"机上，电视屏上出现了一条蓝线。那条线表示脉搏从她的大脑经由脊柱到达手臂。德马克尽可能

rewire *v.* 重装电线　　　　　　　　　　spinal *adj.* 脊柱的

to her arm muscles. DeMichael concentrated as hard as she could. Slowly, she got the line on the TV screen to move up. Still, her arm didn't move. But the line showed that more impulses were reaching her arm. One day, DeMichael got the arm to move. Everyone in the room cheered. She did the same thing with her legs. It took several years, but biofeedback worked. DeMichael learned to walk using just a *cane*.

Western scientists no longer scoff at biofeedback. They see it as a hot new medical tool. It has been used to teach some children how to pay better attention in school. Astronauts use it to fight *motion* sickness during space travel. It has even been used to treat certain forms of cancer. Clearly, biofeedback is here to stay. Bernard Brucker put it this way. "Biofeedback," he says, has opened up a whole new *era* in human learning.

集中心神。慢慢地，她让屏幕上的线向上移动了。她的手臂仍然没有移动。但这条线说明了她的手臂有了更多的脉波。直到有一天，德马克的手臂可以移动了。病房里的每个人都欢呼了起来。她的双腿也同样得到了恢复。这一切花了几年的时间，但"生物回馈"的确奏效了。德马克学会走路了，只借助于一根手杖。

西方的科学家们不再嘲笑"生物回馈"。他们视它为一个先进而热门的医疗工具。"生物回馈"还会用来教孩子们如何在学校里更加集中注意力。宇航员们用"生物回馈"来克制太空之旅时的不良反应。"生物回馈"甚至可用来治疗某种癌症。很明显的是"生物回馈"会一直延续下去。伯纳德·布鲁克说："生物回馈"已经开始了人类学习全新的纪元。"

---

cane *n.* 手杖

motion *n.* 动作；举动

era *n.* 纪元

15

Cryonics: Death on Ice

Like most people, Dick Clair wanted to live a long life. He didn't quite make it, however. At the age of 57, he grew ill and died. But Clair, a TV comedy writer, was determined to have the last laugh. So he arranged to have his body frozen instead of *buried* in the ground. Someday, Clair hoped, scientists would find a *cure* for the disease that killed him. Then doctors could *thaw* out

In the future, whatever disease killed this person being placed in a metal tube may be curable. So he or she has been frozen, using a practice called cryonics. When a cure for the disease is found, the person's body may be thawed out, giving him or her a second chance at life.

冷冻人

在未来，无论因什么疾病而死的人被置于一个金属管里都可能被治愈。运用人体冷冻术，人可以被冷冻。当该疾病的治愈方法被找到时，这个人的身体就会被取出来，这样可以给人第二次生机。

像大多数人一样，迪克·克莱尔想活得长一些。然而，他并没有达成心愿。在57岁的时候，他生病，死掉了。然而克莱尔是一位电视喜剧作家，决定笑到最后。所以，他安排把自己的身体冷冻起来，而不是埋在地下。克莱尔希望有一天科学家们能够找到治愈夺走他性命的疾病的方法。到时候，医生们可以把他的身体解冻，治愈他。一旦苏醒过来，克莱尔就

bury *v.* 埋藏
thaw *v.* 解冻

cure *n.* 疗法

his body and cure him. Once revived, Clair could start writing TV comedy shows again.

Like a growing number of people, Clair believed in *cryonics*. Cryonics is the practice of freezing a body at the moment of death. Cryonic suspension was first done in 1968. Since then, many people have been frozen. Hundreds more have signed up for future freezing. Some even plan to have their favorite dog or cat frozen with them. That way, owner and pet may be *reunited* when a cure is found.

Cryonics takes careful planning. As soon as someone dies, oxygen must be *pumped into* the body. That keeps the body tissues from decaying. The body must also be packed in ice to keep it cool. Then the blood is *drained* and replaced with a special fluid. Next, the body is wrapped in plastic and zipped into a sleeping bag. Finally, the bag is put into a nine-foot metal tube. A special

---

又可以开始写电视喜剧了。

正像越来越多的人一样，克莱尔相信人体冷冻学。人体冷冻学就是在死亡的时刻把身体冷冻起来。第一次人体冷冻是在1968年，其后，很多人都被冷冻过。数百人也都已经报名要在以后被冷冻。一些人甚至打算把他们以后的猫狗和他们一起冷冻。那样的话，主人和宠物就可以在找到治疗方法以后再次重聚。

人体冷冻需要周密的规划。人一死就要马上把氧气注进身体里。那会防止身体组织的腐烂。身体也一定要用冰包好以保持冷却。然后血液被排光用一种特殊的液体取代。下一步，身体用塑料包起来被放进一个睡袋里。最后，袋子被放进9英尺的金属管子里。一种被称为液体氮的特殊冷

---

cryonics *n.* 人体冷冻学
pump into 用泵把……送入

reunite *v.* 重聚
drain *v.* 使(水等)流干；排水

cooling gas, called liquid *nitrogen*, is pumped into the tube. Slowly, the temperature drops all the way to -321 °F. At such a super-low temperature, a body will last almost forever. The decay that would take one second at room temperature would take 30 trillion years at -321°F! So people such as Clair can be kept on ice for a very long time.

Cyronics is not a proven science. There are still plenty of bugs to be worked out. One of the biggest hurdles is the freezing process itself. Parts of a human body can be preserved for a short time. A heart, for example, can be saved for several hours. This has made human heart *transplants* possible. But saving a whole body for a long time is much harder.

Freezing will preserve it. But freezing also tends to destroy it. The human body is made up of cells surrounded by water. As soon as the temperature drops below 32 °F, that water starts to expand. It

---

却气体被注进管道。温度慢慢降到零下321华氏度（零下160摄氏度）。在如此的超低温环境下，身体几乎永远都会维持下去。室温环境下一秒钟便会发生的腐烂在零下321华氏度（零下160摄氏度）要花上300,000亿年。所以像克莱尔一样的人们能够在冰上被保持相当长的一段时间。

人体冷冻术并不是一门被证实的科学，尚有很多缺陷要解决。最大的障碍之一就是冷冻过程本身。人体部位可以被保存一小会，以心脏为例，它能维持几个小时，这让人体心脏移植成为可能。但要想把整个身体维持长时间则困难许多。

冷冻可以保存人的身体，但同样也容易造成伤害。人体是由被水包围的细胞所构成的。一旦温度降到零度以下，水会马上开始膨胀。会形成冰

---

nitrogen *n.* 氮

transplant *v.* 移植

forms ice *crystals*. That causes tearing and damages body tissue. All bodies in cryonic suspension have suffered tissue damage. There is no guarantee that scientists will ever figure out a way to repair the damage.

Let's assume, however, that they do. Let's also assume that scientists solve all the other technical problems. Moral questions would still remain. Who should get frozen?Cryonic suspension is not cheap. At present, it costs more than $100,000. Some people *opt* for a cheaper solution. They pay $35,000 each to have just their heads frozen. They are gambling that scientists will someday be able to attach each head to a brand new body. Still, freezing any part of the body takes big *bucks*. Does that mean only rich people should get a second chance at life?

Surely, not everyone can be frozen. The world already has too

---

凌，那会造成膨胀而破坏身体组织。人体冷冻术的多数人体都发生了组织损坏。也没有谁能保证科学家们会找到办法修复这些破损。

　　然而，让我们假定他们能够找到办法，也能够解决其他的一切技术问题的话。道德问题也依然存在。谁应该被冷冻？冷冻术并不便宜。目前，它要花费至少100,000美元。一些人选择一个便宜一点的方法，他们只花35,000美元把他们的头部冻起来。他们冒险投机，科学家有一天会找出办法把每个头颅都与一个全新的身体连接。可身体的局部冷冻依然花销不菲。难道，这就意味着只有有钱人才应该获得第二次新生吗？

　　当然，并不是每个人都能够被冷冻的。这个世界上已经有太多的人

---

crystal *n.* 结晶
buck *n.* （美俚）元

opt *v.* 选择

many people. What would happen if lots of "dead" people came back to life? The world could not support them all. So someone would have to decide who gets frozen and who doesn't.

Should the young be favored over the old? Should *law-abiding* people be picked over criminals? Would a musician be selected ahead of a street sweeper?

There are other problems as well. Let's suppose a wife dies and is cry-onically suspended. Is her *widower* free to remarry? What happens to her money and property? If she is thawed out, can she move back into her old house? Can she demand her old job back? How would she talk to her kids if she's now 20 or 30 years younger than they are? Suppose she doesn't come back for a thousand years. What would she do in this strange new world? How would she make a living? Who would be her friends?

了。真不知道如果很多"死去的"人都重回人间的话，会发生些什么？地球不可能养活所有人。所以说一定得有人来决定谁被冷冻，而谁不能？

难道年轻人应该比老年人更优先吧？还是遵纪守法之人应比罪犯更优先？一个音乐家会先于一个扫大街的而被选择吗？

此外，还有其他问题。假想一位妻子死后被冷藏，她的丈夫有再婚的自由吗？她的财产又会怎样？如果解冻治愈的话，她能搬回原来的房子吗？能要求重回原来的工作岗位吗？如果现在她比子女还要年轻二三十岁，又应该怎样和他们讲话？假若她1000年都不苏醒，在一个陌生的世界里，她又会如何呢？她会怎样谋生？又和谁交朋友？

---

law-abiding *adj.* 守法的   widower *n.* 鳏夫

The questions go on and on. Still, people cling to the hope that they can someday live again. In 1993 *Omni* magazine held an essay contest. The winner got a free cryonic suspension. *Omni* received hundreds of essays. People gave lots of good reasons for wanting to live again. Some wrote that they were excited about the *distant* future and wanted to see it for themselves. Others wanted to carry knowledge of today's world to the people of the future. Still others felt that they had missed out on things in this life and wanted a second chance. One young reader—the winner—had been injured in a car accident. He wanted to come back "healthy and *healed*."

Cryonics may prove to be a false hope. All the frozen dead bodies may be just that—frozen and dead. But cryonics brings hope to those who believe in it. Even if it doesn't work out, what have they lost besides the money? As Dick Clair once said, "To me, [cryonics] is a way to stay alive."

这些问题一直无人解答，可人们依然梦想着有朝一日自己可以重获新生。1993年，Omni杂志举办了一场论文大赛。胜出者可以获得一次免费的人体冷冻，Omni收到了数百篇文章，人们列出了很多的理由为获新生。一些人写道他们对遥远的未来兴奋不已，想亲眼看见。其他人想把现今的知识带到将来去。还有其他人说他们此生错失了一些东西，想得到第二次机会。一位年轻的读者胜出，他曾在一次车祸中受伤。想"安然无恙地回来。"

人体冷冻术可能会被证实是一个错误的希望。一切被冷冻的死尸也许只是那样而已——冰冷而无生气。但冷冻术为它的信奉者带来了希望。即使它并不奏效，除了金钱他们又损失了什么呢？正如迪克·克莱尔曾经所言："对我来讲，冷冻术是一条重生之路。"

---

distant *adj.* 遥远的

heal *v.* 痊愈

16

Needles That Cure

Everyone knows that feet are good for walking, running, and kicking a soccer ball. But did you know that your feet can also play a role in curing headaches, stomachaches, and toothaches? Some people say you can get rid of these and many other *ailments* just by *jabbing* a needle into your foot.

Could well-placed needles stuck in your body cause your aches and pains to disappear? Those who practice an ancient Chinese treatment called acupuncture believe that is true.

It sounds crazy at first. But according to the ancient art of

---

神针

仔细地把针刺入你的身体能减去你的疼痛吗？这项古老的中国疗法称为针灸，实践者们相信那是真的。

众所周知脚是用来走、跑、踢足球。但你是否知道脚在治头痛、胃痛和牙痛上也能起到一定作用？有些人说，把一根针刺进你的脚里你便可以免于这些和许多其他疾病的痛苦。

这听起来可能很疯狂。但根据古老的针灸术来说，那样做的确有效。

---

ailment *n.* 小病

jab *v.* 刺；戳

acupuncture, it works. A needle stuck into a specific point on your second toe can *banish* headaches. A needle between your second and third toe can rid you of a sore throat. A needle put into the outside of your foot can *stimulate* your vision.

Acupuncture began in China more than four thousand years ago. It is based on the belief that there is a natural flow of energy inside each human being. This energy, or life force, is called qi (pronounced CHEE). The qi is said to flow along certain pathways in the body. These *pathways*, called meridians, are like rivers. When they flow freely, you feel strong and healthy. But if one of your meridians gets blocked, the flow of energy is disrupted. Your qi becomes unbalanced. Too much qi builds up in one part of your body. Other parts don't get enough. That's where the needles come in. By inserting needles in just the right spots, you can unblock your

---

把一根针刺入你第二根脚趾会减除你的头痛。刺入第二根、第三根脚趾之间的位置能治喉痛。把针刺入你脚的外侧又可以提高视力。

针灸术在四千多年前起源于中国。它是构建在一个基础观点之上，认为每个人身体里都有个自然的能量流脉。这种能量或生命力称为气，说气是沿着某些特定的通道在人体中流动的。这种通道称为经脉，就像河流一样，当流通顺畅时，你就会感觉很强健。但如果某一条经脉堵塞了，体能流便会中断，你的气便会变得紊乱。过多的气在你的身体的某个部位聚集，其他部位便会能量不足。针灸就从那里而入，把针刺入合适的位置，

---

acupuncture *n.* 针刺疗法
stimulate *v.* 刺激

banish *v.* 消除
pathway *n.* 途径

meridians and get your qi flowing correctly again.

No one has ever been able to prove the existence of these energy pathways. But over the years Chinese *practitioners* have fine-tuned their view of qi. They have identified 14 meridians. They have named about 1,500 points on the body where these meridians can get clogged. And they have figured out which points need to be opened to relieve different pains. Let's say your immune system is weak. In that case you'll need a needle put in near your elbow. But if *nausea* is your problem, the needle must go lower down on your arm, right near your *wrist*.

When people in Europe and America first heard about acupuncture, they were skeptical. For a long time they paid no attention to stories about it. But by the 1970s some doctors were taking a closer look. Some of them began to experiment with it. What

---

就可以打通你的脉络，让你的气重新流通。

没人曾经证实这些能量通道存在与否，但这么多年来，中国的针灸实践者已经验证了他们对关于气的观点。他们已经确认了14条经络，命名了1500个经络可能阻塞的点。并且已经找出了哪些结点需要打通，来解除不同的病痛。假设你的免疫系统较弱。针需要刺入你的肘部附近。但如果你晕船作呕的话，针就要刺在你手臂偏下的位置上了，就在手腕附近。

当欧洲美洲的人们首次听说针灸的时候，很是怀疑。很长时间里他们对关于针灸的故事传闻毫无关注。但到20世纪70年代，一些医生开始更密切关注了。有一些人开始做实验。结果让他们吃了一惊，很多病人都说

---

meridian *n.* 顶点
nausea *n.* 晕船

practitioner *n.* 从业者
wrist *n.* 手腕

WEIRD SCIENCE

they found surprised them. Many patients said that acupuncture *lessened* their pain. When nothing else would work, it often gave them relief.

One woman was suffering from asthma. Her doctor gave her medicine, but it made her body swell up like a balloon. Soon she weighed 300 pounds. Still, the *asthma* attacks kept coming. As soon as she started acupuncture treatment, though, the asthma went away. The woman lost 80 pounds and was able to throw away all her asthma medicine.

Another patient had neck pain that she could not shake. After a year of misery, she turned to acupuncture. "All of a sudden, the pain was gone," she said.

Does this mean that the Chinese view of energy pathways is accurate? Maybe not. Western doctors have another theory about

---

针灸的确减缓了病痛。当其他疗法都不奏效时，针灸法通常可以给病人以病痛的解脱。

有一位女患者深受哮喘病折磨，医生给她开了药。但结果她的身体却像气球一样地肿胀了起来。不久她便重达300磅。而哮喘的症状却并无好转的迹象。可刚一采用针灸疗法，哮喘症状就都消失了。这位病人体重减掉了80磅，也能够丢下所有的哮喘药物了。

另一位病人脖子疼得不能转动。在忍受一年的病痛之后，她求助于针灸。她说："突然间，疼痛都不见了。"

莫非这就意味着中国人有关能量通道的观念都是准确无误的？或许并不如此。西方的医生对针灸为何奏效有另一套理论。他们发现把针刺进身

---

lessen *v.* 减少；减轻   asthma *n.* 哮喘

104

why acupuncture works. They have found that sticking needles into the body can stimulate the nervous system. The *nervous* system then releases chemicals into your body. Many doctors think it is these chemicals that take away the pain.

Some people have said that acupuncture is all in your head. That is, it only works because you expect it to work. But that would not explain why it works on animals. Cows, dogs, cats, and horses have all been helped by acupuncture. And certainly these animals were not true believers!

Acupuncture has also worked on many humans who didn't think it would. One such patient was Zang-Hee Cho. Cho was a California physicist. In 1993 he fell while hiking on a mountain. He hurt his back so badly he could barely walk. Some of his relatives said he should try acupuncture, but he *scoffed* at the idea. He didn't think there was

体可以刺激神经系统。神经系统会向你的身体里释放出化学物。很多医生认为是这些化学物消除了病痛。

一些人曾说针灸只是在你的头脑里而已。也就是说，它能奏效只是因为你期待它那样而已。但这并不能解释它如何能起效于动物之上，牛、狗、猫、马全都曾受益于针灸。而这些动物当然不可能信仰针灸术。

针灸术还奏效于许多对其并不信任的人。周仓喜是位加州的物理学家。1993年，他在山上远足时跌倒了。后背摔得非常严重，以致他几乎不能走动了。一些家人劝说他应该试试针灸，可他却对其嗤之以鼻。他并

nervous *adj.* 精神系统的 scoff *v.* 嘲笑

anything to it. When he finally agreed to give it a try, he was amazed. "After about 10 minutes I felt the pain *melting* away," he said.

Cho later set up a study to find out how acupuncture affects the brain. He watched needles being put into patients' feet. The goal was to *unclog* the qi that flowed to the eyes. That sounded like nonsense to Cho. But then he took pictures of the patients' brains during the *procedure*. He was shocked. Their brains showed the same activity as when a light was shone in their eyes. "I never thought anything would happen," Cho said. "But it's very clear that stimulating the acupuncture point triggers activity in the visual *cortex* [part of the brain]."

Other studies have found that acupuncture increases the flow of blood to the brain. It sends more blood to the part of the brain that registers pain. Thanks to studies like these, more and more people are lining up for treatment. The World Health Organization has even

不认为针灸会怎样。但当他最终同意试一试时，他震惊了。他说："大约十分钟后，我感到疼痛逐渐消散了。"

后来，周开始调查研究针灸是如何影响大脑的。他亲眼观察针被刺入病人的双脚，目的是打通流向眼睛的气。对周来讲，那听起来非常荒谬。但当他在过程中给病人大脑拍照后，他震惊了。病人的大脑体现出与当一束光线射到眼睛上所导致的相同的活动。周说："我从未想到会发生些什么事情。但是非常明显对针灸点的刺激的确会引发大脑视觉皮层的活动。"

其他研究也发现针灸可以增加大脑的血液流量。向大脑中记载疼痛的部位输入更多的血液。由于这些研究，越来越多的人准备接受针灸治疗。世界卫生组织甚至已经起草了一份针灸可以治疗的疾病列单。这张表单包

melt *v.* 使渐渐消失

procedure *n.* 过程

unclog *v.* 使畅通

cortex *n.* 皮质

drawn up a list of ailments that can be treated this way. The list has everything from chest infections to *earaches* to back pain.

If you should ever try acupuncture, here's what you will find. Up to 20 or more needles will be stuck into various parts of your body. These needles are very thin, and most patients say they don't cause much pain. Some of the needles may not be pushed in very far. But others may be put as deep as three inches. The needles will stay in place for 15 to 30 minutes. Practitioners say you might feel relief right away or you might need several *sessions* to feel better.

One word of warning: In most states, acupuncturists don't need medical degrees. So if you think your qi is out of line, be careful. Pick someone who knows what he or she is doing. A bad acupuncturist could damage your nerves or *puncture* your *lung*. If that were to happen, you'd be in worse shape than you were when you started.

含了一切从胸腔感染到耳痛再到背痛。

如果你尝试针灸的话，你会发现20根或更多的针会被刺入你身体不同部位。这些针非常细，大多数病人说并不很痛。一些不会被刺的很深，而另一些则会被刺入深达3英尺。会维持15到30分钟。实践者说你可能会立即感到疼痛减轻，也可能需要几个周期才会好转。

有一点要注意的是：在美国大多数州内，针灸医生并不需要医学学位。如果你认为自己的气乱的话，要小心了。一定要选一位懂行的人。一位不称职的针灸师可能会使你的神经破损或刺穿你的肺脏。如果真这样的话，那样会比你针灸之前还糟。

---

earache *n.* 耳痛　　　　　　　　session *n.* 聚集在一起的一段时间
puncture *v.* 刺穿　　　　　　　　lung *n.* 肺

Strange Lights over Texas

Marfa, Texas, is a quiet little town. During the day, it seems like any other town in West Texas. But just wait until the sun goes down. That's when things get *spooky*. Something strange happens here at night. No one knows why. And no one knows how. But it's been going on for more than 100 years.

Shown here is a roadside sign along a highway in Marfa, Texas. It directs tourists to a viewing area where they can see the strange lights that appear in the sky over Marfa.

About an hour after the sun sets, lights *appear* in the sky. They

得州上空的神秘之光

这是一块立在得州的马尔法高速公路的路边告示牌。它指示旅游者到一个观赏区去，这样他们就能看到出现在马尔法天空中的怪光了。

得克萨斯州的马尔法是一个安静的小镇。白天的时候就和所有得州西部的城镇一样，但等到太阳下山之后，此时这个小镇就变得有些吓人了。这里的夜晚会发生些奇怪的事情。没人知道为什么，也没人知道是怎么发生的，但这种情况已经持续了一百多年。

日落大约一个小时之后，天穹上就有光出现。它们通常出现在同一个

spooky *adj.* 幽灵般的   appear *v.* 出现

108

always show up in the same place. They are not right over the town. They are off to the south. But they can be seen for miles around.

Nothing about these lights makes sense. One minute their light is soft, but the next minute it is bright. The lights don't come out every night. In fact, there is no way to know when they will show up. The time of year doesn't matter. Neither does the weather. They come on clear nights and cloudy nights. They come when it's hot and when it's *cool*. They come when the air is still. They come when the wind is *blowing*. They even come in the pouring rain.

Sometimes these lights seem to hang in the air. Sometimes they *spin* or dive. They dance from spot to spot. They flash on and off. Sometimes one light breaks into two. At times they seem to be headed straight toward Marfa. At other times they seem to be

---

地方，不在小镇的正上方，而更往南一些，从几英里之外就能看得到它们。

这光本身也并不说明什么，前一分钟还很柔和，后一分钟就变得很明亮。这光并不是每晚都会出现，事实上，人们没办法知道它们什么时候会出现。季节不是决定性因素，天气也不是。它们出现在晴朗和阴云密布的夜晚，出现在炎热和寒冷的日子，平静无风的时候它们也会出现，刮着大风的时候它们也会出现，甚至伴随着倾盆大雨而来。

有时候这些光看起来是悬在空中的，有时候它们盘旋着或是俯冲下来。它们舞蹈般跳来跳去，忽明忽暗。有时候一道光会分裂成两道。有时候它们看起来向着马尔法冲来。其他的时候它们看上去好像飞向远处。这

---

cool *adj.* 凉爽的   blow *v.* 吹
spin *v.* 旋转

running away. The lights also change colors. They may be white. They may be red. They may be green, *pink*, blue, or yellow.

They are called the Ghost Lights of Marfa. Some people think they really are the work of a *ghost*. Back in the 1860s, an Apache Indian chief was killed near Marfa. Some people say his ghost lives on. They say the lights come from his ghost as it wanders through the night. "Nobody's been able to say it isn't so," says Alma Cabezuela.

That may be. But most people don't believe in ghosts. So they have to look for answers somewhere else. If a ghost isn't behind the lights, then what is?

Some people think the lights come from cars. There are roads near the place where the lights appear. But there is a problem with this answer. The lights have been seen since the 1880s. That was

---

些光也会变换颜色，它们可能是白的，可能是红的；它们可能是绿的，粉的，蓝的或者是黄的。

它们被人们称为马尔法的幽灵之光，有人认为它们真的是幽灵所为。回到19世纪60年代，一个阿帕切族的印第安酋长在马尔法附近被杀。有人说他的灵魂还在世间游走，而这光就是他的幽灵在夜晚乱逛的时候发出的。"没人能否定这一点。"阿尔玛·卡博祖拉说。

可能是这样，但大多数人并不相信有幽灵存在。所以他们只好另寻答案。如果这光的来源不是幽灵，那会是什么呢？

有人认为这光来自于汽车。怪光出现的附近有很多道路。但这个答案有一个问题，这光在19世纪80年代就出现了，这远远地早于得州有第一

---

pink *adj.* 粉红色

ghost *n.* 幽灵

MCGRAW-HILL

long before the first car came to Texas.

Could the lights be from fires? Robert Ellison thought they could be. Ellison was the first person to talk *openly* about the lights. He saw them one night in 1883. He was taking care of his cows at the time. Ellison tried to chase the lights on his horse. He couldn't catch them. Later he wondered whether the lights had come from *campfires*. He talked to people who lived in Marfa. It turned out that they had been seeing the lights for years. They, too, had thought of fires. They had even gone out and looked around. But they had never found any sign of fire.

One answer might be that the lights are made by gas. That makes sense. A certain kind of gas sometimes comes from rotting plants. As the gas *floats* up toward the sky, it can blow up. It can turn

---

辆汽车的时间。

　　这光是来自火光吗？罗伯特·艾利森认为有这种可能。艾利森是第一个能大胆讨论这些光的人。他于1883年的一个晚上看到了它们，当时他正在照顾他的奶牛。艾利森企图骑马去追这些光，但他没能追上它们。后来他猜想这些光可能是露营的篝火。他和住在马尔法的人讲了这件事，结果发现这些光已经出现过好多年了。他们也都猜是火光，他们甚至出去四处寻找，但是从未找到任何火的痕迹。

　　一个答案是这光可能是由气体产生。这很有道理，有时候腐烂的植物会产生一种气体。随着这种气体飘向天空，它可能会爆炸，会变成火球。

---

openly *adv.* 公开地
float *v.* 飘浮

campfire *n.* 营火会；营火

into balls of fire. But no gas has been found where the lights appear.

Could there be something strange about the air in Marfa? That's what some people think. They believe there might be some air pocket here that is bending moonlight back toward Earth. That sounds good. But no one has been able to find this air pocket.

Scientists are no help. They keep coming to Marfa. They bring special *tools*. They take pictures of the sky. They watch the lights for weeks at a time. Still, they have found no answer. They agree that the lights are real. But they don't know what makes them.

That is okay with most people in Marfa. They like having a mystery in town. After all, they aren't afraid of the lights. "These lights are *mild*," says the mayor of the town. "They are friendly."

但是在这光出现的地方并没有找到任何气体。

会不会是马尔法的空气中有什么奇怪的物质呢？有些人就是这么想的。它们认为那里可能存在某些气陷，能改变月光的方向并投向地球。这种解释听起来很有道理，但是没人能找到这种气陷。

科学家也没帮上什么忙，他们接二连三地来到马尔法，带着专用的工具。他们给天空拍照，连续几周看着那些光。但他们仍然没找到答案。他们一致同意这光是真的，但他们不知道它们是怎么形成的。

对马尔法的大多数人来说这一切都很正常。他们喜欢镇里有个未解之谜。不管怎么说，他们并不怕这些光。"这些光很温和，"镇长说。"他们很友好，并不会伤害任何人。"

---

tool *n.* 工具

mild *adj.* 温和的

They're not going to *hurt* anybody."

Some people do find the lights *scary*. But they also think the lights are fun. One man tells how he saw the lights while flying his plane on a dark night. "You haven't lived until you have seen the Marfa lights," he says. "That will make the hair on the back of your neck curl."

People come from around the world to see the lights. That brings a lot of money into the town. Maybe that's why people in Marfa like the lights so much. "I have no idea what the lights are," says Marfa's Connie Brisbin. "And, like most people in town, we don't want to know. We're just glad they're here."

Another woman in town agrees. "The Marfa lights are a *mystery*," she says. "Let them stay a mysery."

有些人确实觉得这光很吓人，也认为这光很有趣。有个人描述了他在漆黑的夜晚飞行时看到这光的情形。"你要是没见过马尔法的光简直就白活了，"他说。"看到这些光后你会感到很平静。"

人们从世界各地来到这里看这些光，这给小镇带来了不少收入。也许这就是马尔法的人这么喜欢这光的原因。"我不知道这些光是什么，"马尔法的卡耐·布里斯宾说，"另外，和镇里的大多数人一样，我们也不想知道。我们很高兴能有这些光。"

镇里的另一个女人附和着，"马尔法的光是一个谜，"她说，"就让它一直保持神秘吧。"

---

hurt *v.* 伤害　　　　　　　　　　　　scary *adj.* 吓人的；害怕的
mystery *n.* 神秘；秘密

18

The Lost Dutchman's Mine

Would you like to be rich—really rich? If your answer is yes, here's what you need to do. Go to Arizona. Head east from Phoenix, toward the *Superstition* Mountains. In these hills there is a *gold* mine. It is called the Lost Dutchman's Mine. Some people say it is the richest mine in the world. If you find it, the gold inside could be yours.

Shown here is the Weaver's Needle, a peak in the Superstition Mountains of Arizona. The Lost Dutchman's Mine might be hidden in this area.

荷兰人消失的矿藏

这是亚利桑那州的迷信山脉的顶峰——海狸针。荷兰人消失的矿藏也许就藏在这个地区。

你愿意富有吗——是真的很富有？如果你的答案是肯定的，你就该这么做：去亚利桑那州，从凤凰城向东走，向着迷信山脉。在群山中有一个金矿，被称作荷兰人消失的矿藏。有人说那是世界上最富饶的矿藏。如果你能找到它，那里的金子就都是你的。

superstition *n.* 迷信   gold *adj.* 金的

Doesn't that sound good? But don't pack your bags just yet. There is some bad news. People have looked for this mine for many years. No one has been able to find it. Some people have lost all their money looking for it. Others have lost their lives.

The story of the mine begins with Jacob Waltz. Sometime around 1840, he moved from Europe to the United States. No one knows the year for sure. There are other things about Waltz that are not *definite*. But we do know he lived in California. He spent a long time looking for gold there. He didn't have much *luck*. So in 1863 Waltz moved to Arizona.

When he got there, Waltz went on looking for gold. For 10 years he found nothing. But one day his luck changed—or so the story goes. It is said that Waltz was in a bar with his friend Jacob Weisner

---

听起来是不是不错？但别急着收拾行装。还有一些坏消息。人们已经找了很多年了，但没人能找到它。有些人花了全部的钱去找它，另一些人则丢了性命。

矿藏的故事开始于雅格布·沃尔兹。大约在1840年，他从欧洲搬到了美国。没人知道确切的年份。还有其他关于沃尔兹的事情并不确切，但我们确定他住在加利福尼亚州。他在那儿花了很长的时间去找金子，但他不怎么走运，所以在1863年沃尔兹搬到了亚利桑那州。

沃尔兹到了那儿便开始继续找金子，10年过去了他什么也没找到。但有一天他转运了——或者说故事是这么说的。据说沃尔兹和他的朋友雅

---

definite *adj.* 一定的

luck *n.* 运气

when a fight *broke out*. Waltz and Weisner stopped the fight. They saved the life of a young Mexican named Miguel Peralta. The Peralta family wanted to thank them. So the Peraltas told Waltz and Weisner about a *secret* gold mine. It wasn't just any old mine. It turned out to have more gold in it than Waltz or Weisner could believe.

The two men began to work the *mine*. But one day, Apache Indians appeared. They killed Weisner. We don't know why. But it scared Jacob Waltz. He left the mountains and went to live in Phoenix. First, though, he covered up the entrance to the mine. He made sure no one else would see it.

For a long time, Waltz told no one about the mine. From time to time he did *sneak* back to it, but he only dug up enough gold to live on for a while.

格布·韦斯纳在酒吧，遇到一群人在打架。沃尔兹和韦斯纳制止了这场打架。他们救了一个名叫米格尔·佩拉尔塔的年轻的墨西哥人。佩拉尔塔一家想要感谢他们，因此佩拉尔塔家人告诉了沃尔兹和韦斯纳秘密金矿的事。那并不是什么普通的旧矿，实际上沃尔兹和韦斯纲发现那儿的金子多得超出了他们的想象。

于是两个人就开始开矿。但有一天，阿帕切族的印第安人出现了，他们杀了韦斯纳。我们不知道原因。但这吓坏了雅格布·沃尔兹。他离开了群山到凤凰城去居住。他首先掩藏好了金矿的入口，确保没有其他人能看到。

过了很长一段时间，沃尔兹没对任何人提到这个金矿。他不时地溜回去，但他只挖出了足够他生活一段时间的所需要的金子。

---

break out 爆发
mine *n.* 矿

secret *adj.* 秘密的
sneak *v.* 偷偷地走

In Phoenix, Waltz bought a small farm and *raised* chickens. He became friends with a woman who ran a *store*. Her name was Julia Thomas. In 1891 Thomas ran short of money. It looked as if she might lose her store. Waltz wanted to help. He told Thomas about the mine. Until then, Thomas had thought of Waltz as a poor chicken farmer. But now Waltz *pulled out* a piece of gold and showed it to her. "There's a great deal more where that came from," he said.

Waltz *promised* to take Thomas to the mine. They made plans to go. But by this time, Waltz was an old man. Before they could leave, he became sick and died.

Waltz died without telling anyone where the mine was. But he left behind some clues. Just before he died, Waltz wrote, "No miner will ever find my mine." Then he added, "To find my mine you must pass a cow barn. It can't be seen from the trail, but I can see the trail from

在凤凰城，沃尔兹买了一间小农场养鸡，他和一个开商店的女人成了朋友。她的名字叫作朱莉亚·托马斯。1891年，托马斯的钱快用完了。看情况她不能再经营商店了。沃尔兹想要帮忙，他告诉了托马斯金矿的事。在那之前，托马斯一直以为沃尔兹是一个贫穷的养鸡的农民。但沃尔兹拿出了一块金子给她看。"这样东西在开凿地还有的是。"他说。

沃尔兹答应带托马斯去那个金矿。他们做好了计划。但那时候沃尔兹已经是个老人了。没等他们出发，他就生病死了。

沃尔兹死前没有告诉任何人金矿在哪儿，但他留下了一些线索，就在他临死前，他写道，"没有矿工能找到我的金矿。"接着他又加上一句，"要想找到它得先经过一个养奶牛的牛棚，在路上看不到我的金矿，但我

raise *v.* 饲养；养育　　store *n.* 商店
pull out 退出；拉出　　promise *v.* 答应；许诺

my mine." Waltz threw in a few more *clues* as well. Here are two of them:

"If you pass three red hills, you have gone too far."

"Across from the mine is a cave."

It wasn't much to go on. But that didn't stop people from trying to find the mine. Over the years, thousands of gold hunters have gone to the Superstition Mountains. The first person to go was Julia Thomas herself. After a few weeks, she gave up. She needed money, so she printed and sold maps to the Lost Dutchman's Mine. She did not know where it was, of course. Still, people bought her maps.

The story of the mine *spread* around the world. People rushed to Arizona. They all hoped to find the mine. Many spent years looking. But none found it. Some went broke, and some ended up dead.

Dr. Adolph Ruth is one of those who lost their lives looking for the

---

从金矿能看到小路。"沃尔兹又留下了几条线索。以下是其中的两条：

"如果你过了三座红色的小山，你就走得太远了。"

"在金矿的对面是一个山洞。"

没有太大的价值，但这并没有阻止人们试着去寻找金矿。数以千计的淘金者年复一年地来到迷信山脉。第一个去的人就是朱莉亚·托马斯本人。几周后，她就放弃了。她需要钱，因此她印制并卖掉了寻找荷兰人消失的矿藏的地图。当然她并不知道它在哪儿，但人们仍然买她的地图。

金矿的故事传到了世界各地，人们蜂拥到亚利桑那州，都想要找到金矿。很多人花了许多年来寻找，但没人能找到。有些人破产了，有些人死了。

阿道夫·鲁思博士是为了寻找荷兰人消失的矿藏而丧命的人之一。

---

clue *n.* 线索　　　　　　　　　　　　　spread *v.* 传播

THE LOST DUTCHMAN'S MINE

Lost Dutchman's Mine. Ruth set out in 1931. No one knows what happened. But somewhere in the mountains, he was killed. His head was cut off. Another person died while looking for the mine 16 years later. This time the man's name was James Cravey. Many other men have died *mysterious* deaths in these same mountains. Has someone been trying to keep people from finding the mine? Or are the deaths accidental?

No one knows. In fact, we still don't know whether the Lost Dutchman's Mine is real. As time has passed, people have *made up* their own clues. Lies have been mixed in with the truth. It has grown harder and harder to tell which is which. But as one man says, "Don't let the truth stand in the way of a good story." So if you're looking to get rich quick, you might want to make that trip to Arizona after all.

鲁思于1931出发，没人知道发生了什么，但在山里的某处，他被杀了。他的头被砍了下来。16年后另一个人也在寻找矿藏的过程中死了，这一次这个人的名字叫作詹姆斯·科雷威。另外也有很多人神秘的死在同一片山里。是不是有人想要阻止人们寻找金矿呢？还是这些死亡都属意外？

没人知道。事实上，我们仍然不知道荷兰人消失的矿藏是不是真的。随着时间流逝，人们编造出了他们自己的线索。谎言和真相交织在了一起，变得越来越难分辨。但正如一个人所说的，"不要因为真相而放弃一个美好的故事。"所以如果你希望快速发财，你也许还应该到亚利桑那州一游。

---

mysterious *adj.* 神秘的　　　　　　　　　　　　make up　组成

The Missing Divers

It was going to be a great day. The four Canadians felt sure of that. On November 4, 1994, they *gathered* in Florida. They had come to fish and dive in the Gulf of Mexico. Jeff Wandich had a boat. So he and Kent Munro, Omar Shearer, and Dave Madott set out on the boat. They *planned* to be back by dark. But they did not make it. In fact, only one of the men ever made it back.

Shown here are the three Canadian divers who disappeared in the Gulf of Mexico. A Web site has been set up about these divers at www.vanished.org.

消失的潜水员

这是消失在墨西哥湾的三个加拿大潜水员。为了这些潜水员人们建立了一个网站www.vanished.org。

这将会是一个重大的日子，4个加拿大人对此深信无疑。1994年11月4日，他们聚集在弗洛里达州，到墨西哥湾钓鱼和潜水。杰·万迪奇有一条船。于是他和肯特·芒罗、奥马尔·希勒和戴夫·马多特乘船出发了。他们计划在天黑前回来。但他们却没能回来，事实上，最终只有一个人回来了。

---

gather *v.* 聚集　　　　　　　　　　　　　　　　plan *v.* 计划

About 60 miles out, Jeff stopped the boat. From here, they could dive 129 feet down. They could get to an old ship that lay at the bottom of the ocean. The water was getting *rough*. The *waves* were more than three feet high. But the men weren't worried. They had dived in bad weather before. They put on diving suits and broke into pairs. Jeff dived with Dave, and Omar dived with Kent.

By the time they were finished diving, something was wrong with the boat. It was filling with water. The men couldn't save it. They jumped into the water and hung onto a rope, hoping someone would come along and save them. No one did. Four hours later, at 7 p.m., their boat sank.

The men knew they were in trouble. Still, they tried to think clearly. There was a light *tower* about four miles away. They could see its lights flashing on and off. If they could swim to it, they could save themselves.

开出60英里之后，杰夫停了船。在这个地方他们能够潜到水下129英尺，他们可以到一艘停在海底的旧船上去。海水开始变得汹涌，海浪有三尺多高。但这些人并不担心，他们之前也曾在恶劣的天气情况下潜水。他们穿上潜水服，两两一组。杰夫与戴维一组，奥马尔和肯特一组。

他们潜水归时，船有些不对劲，里面装满了水。他们没办法救船，便跳进水里，紧紧抓住一根绳子，希望有人能出现并解救他们，但是没人来。4个小时之后，即晚上7:00，船沉了。

他们知道他们遇到麻烦了，但他们仍然努力保持清醒。在4英里外有一个灯塔，他们能看到它的灯光闪烁。如果他们能游过去，他们就得救了。

rough *adj.* 粗野的　　　　　　　　　　wave *n.* 波浪
tower *n.* 塔

Omar wasn't sure he could make it. He didn't think he could swim that far.

"Omar, we don't have a choice," Dave told him. "We'll make it. We'll all make it."

With those brave words, the four friends began swimming.

"We just *plugged along*," Jeff later said, "side by side, with me on one end and Dave on the other, Omar and Kent between us."

After five minutes, Jeff felt fear washing over him. "I had tears in my eyes," he later said. He turned away so his friends would not see him cry. He swam away from them for a minute to pull himself together.

"I wasn't far away from them," he said, "maybe 10 feet, two waves away, and then I took a look to my left." Jeff didn't see them *anymore*. They were gone.

奥马尔不确定自己能不能做到，他觉得自己游不了那么远。

"奥马尔，我们别无选择。"戴维对他说，"我们会做到的。我们都会做到的。"

听了这些勇敢的话语，4个伙伴开始游泳。

"我们是在拼命。"后来杰夫说。"一个挨着一个，我在这头，戴维在另一头，奥马尔和肯特在我们中间。"

5分钟之后，杰夫感觉恐惧笼罩了他。"我的眼里含着泪水。"后来他说。他转过头去，好让他的朋友们看不到他在哭。他游开了一分钟，让自己冷静一下。

"我离他们并不远。"他说，"大概十英尺，就在两个浪头开外，然后我看了一眼我的左边。"杰夫没有再看到他们，他们不见了。

---

plug along 拼命做某事   anymore *adv.* 再也不

Jeff couldn't believe it. Where could they be? He called to them and thought he heard them answer. But he could not see them. By this time, the waves were about four feet high. He thought the waves were keeping him from seeing them. In any case, he knew they were all headed for the light tower. So he turned toward it and began swimming again.

For the next four hours, Jeff swam through the waves and the wind. He tried not to think about sharks. He was *exhausted*. But he kept swimming. At last he reached the tower. He *climbed up* onto it, hoping his friends might already be there. They weren't. Jeff thought they would come soon. As the hours passed, he thought a boat must have saved them. At last, after 35 hours on the tower, he was picked up by the Coast Guard. That's when he learned that his friends were still missing.

杰夫不能相信。他们能去哪儿呢？他呼喊他们，并且认为他听到了回答。但他看不到他们。这时候，浪已经有4英尺高了。他觉得是因为海浪他才看不到他们。不管怎么说，他知道他们都在朝着灯塔游去。所以他朝向灯塔开始游去。

之后的4个小时，杰夫穿过了海浪和狂风。他努力不想鲨鱼。他累得筋疲力尽，但他一直游着，最终他到达了灯塔。他爬上去，希望他的朋友们已经到这儿了。但他们没有。杰夫以为他们很快就到。随着时间流逝，他觉得肯定是有船救了他们。最后，在塔上呆了35个小时之后，他被海岸巡逻队救起，这时他才知道他的朋友们一直在失踪状态。

---

exhausted *adj.* 疲惫的   climb up 爬上去

The Coast Guard looked all over for Omar, Kent, and Dave. They used planes and boats. They used their best tools. It was one of the biggest *searches* ever in the Gulf of Mexico. It covered 23,000 square miles of sea. But no bodies were found. After six days, the Coast Guard gave up.

The families of the missing men did not want to give up. They promised $300,000 to anyone who would help them find the men. They gave people money just to keep looking. But it did no good. Omar Shearer, Dave Madott, and Kent Munro were gone.

How could this be? The water was warm. The men were young and strong, and they all knew how to swim. None of them had been sick or hurt, and they were all wearing *special* clothes to help them float. So it does not seem likely they all drowned. Even if they did, their bodies would have floated. Surely the Coast Guard would have

---

海岸巡逻队四处寻找奥马尔、肯特和戴维。他们动用了飞机和船只，用最好的工具。这是墨西哥湾有史以来最大的一次搜索之一，包括了23,000平方英里的海域。但是没有找到尸体。6天之后，海岸巡逻队放弃了。

失踪者的家人不想放弃，他们悬赏300,000美元给能找到他们的人。他们雇人继续寻找。但是没有用。奥马尔·希勒、戴夫·马多特和肯特·芒罗不见了。

这怎么可能呢？海水很温暖。这些人年轻而强壮，而且都会游泳。没有人生病或者受伤了，而且都穿着能帮助他们漂浮的特殊服装。所以他们不可能都淹死了。即使是这样，他们的尸体会浮上来，海岸巡逻队就应该

---

search *n.* 搜索　　　　　　　　　　special *adj.* 专门的

found one of these floating bodies.

Did sharks devour the men? Scientists say no. There were not many sharks in this part of the ocean. There were some. But they weren't the kind that goes after people. Besides, *sharks* wouldn't eat the men's special diving clothes. So pieces of these clothes should have been found.

Was Jeff lying? Did he kill his friends or lie about what happened to them? That is hard to believe because he loved these men. They had been friends for years. And to prove that he was telling the *truth*, he took a lie detector test. This test tells whether someone is lying. "The kid passed with flying colors," said one man. "He was telling the truth."

能发现一具漂浮的尸体。

是鲨鱼吞食了这些人吗？科学家说不是。这片大洋没有多少鲨鱼。是有一些，但不是会追捕人类的那种。另外，鲨鱼不会吃掉人类的特制潜水服，所以应该会发现这些衣服的碎片。

是杰夫在撒谎吗？是不是他杀了他的朋友们或者对发生在他们身上的事撒了谎？这真是难以相信，因为他很爱他的朋友们，他们已经做了很多年的朋友。而且为了证明他说的是真话，他接受了测谎仪测试，这个测试可以分辨一个人是不是在撒谎。"他成功地通过了测试，"一个人说，"他说的是实话。"

---

shark *n.* 鲨鱼　　　　　　　　　　　truth *n.* 事实

Some people think a boat picked up Kent, Omar, and Dave. Many people sneak through the Gulf of Mexico to buy and sell *drugs*. Did one of these people kill the men? Or *kidnap* them? Or give them a lift? Did the three men run off and start lives in some other country?

Years later, we still don't know what happened. The families of the missing men keep hoping for answers. But none has been found. The question is still there: What happened to Kent Munro, Omar Shearer, and Dave Madott?

有的人认为有船救了奥马尔、肯特和戴维。很多人会从墨西哥湾偷渡出境买卖毒品。是不是这些人杀了他们？或者是绑架了他们？或者搭救了他们，是不是这三个人逃到了其他国家生活？

很多年后，我们仍不知道发生了什么。失踪人员的家人仍在期待答案。但是没有什么发现。疑问仍然在：到底肯特·芒罗、奥马尔·希勒和戴夫·马多特发生了什么？

---

drug *n.* 毒品；药   kidnap *v.* 绑架

20

Death by Anthrax

Something was wrong. Kathy Nguyen (new-win) felt terrible. She was cold. She was tired. Every part of her body hurt. And she could not stop *coughing*. For two days the 61-year-old Nguyen tried to keep going. She showed up for work at the Manhattan Eye, Ear and Throat Hospital in New York. But by the third day, her heart was racing. She found it hard to *breathe*. At

The poster on this column shows a picture of Kathy Nguyen, who died from anthrax. Police put it up hoping someone might know how Nguyen got the anthrax.

炭疽热引发的死亡

这一栏的海报上是一张凯西·古颜的照片，她死于炭疽病。警察张贴了这张海报，希望有人会知道古颜是怎样染上炭疽热的。

出了什么事情了，凯西·古颜觉得很难受。她很冷，很累，身体的每个部位都疼，而且她不停地咳嗽。61岁的古颜回到纽约的曼哈顿眼耳喉医院上班，坚持了两天。但到了第三天，她的心脏跳得飞快，感到很难呼

---

cough *v.* 咳嗽

breathe *v.* 呼吸

last, she asked a friend to take her to a *hospital.*

Doctors thought there might be a problem with Nguyen's heart. But tests showed that was not true. After three days, doctors found out what was really wrong. But by then it was too late. The next day, Kathy Nguyen died. A *disease* called anthrax had killed her.

A disease is a sickness. The *anthrax* disease is caused by bacteria. People get sick if they even touch anthrax *bacteria*. They get sick if they breathe in the bacteria. These bacteria are rare. Most of us never come near them. But in the fall of 2001, when Nguyen died, they were a big problem. That's because someone was using them to kill people.

Nguyen's death came just a few weeks after September 11,

吸。最后，她请一个朋友带他去医院。

医生们认为可能是古颜的心脏有问题，但是测试结果表示并不是这样。3天后，医生发现了真正的病因，但那时候已经太晚了。第二天，凯西·古颜死了，死于一种叫作炭疽热的疾病。

疾病是一种不健康的状态，炭疽热疾病是由细菌引起的。人们一旦触碰到炭疽杆菌就会生病，如果吸入了这种细菌也会生病。这种病菌很稀少，绝大多数人从未靠近过它。但在2001年的秋天，当古颜死后，它们就成了一个大问题，因为有人在利用它们杀人。

古颜的死于2001年9月11日的几周后。在那一天，恐怖主义者杀死上

---

hospital *n.* 医院

anthrax *n.* 炭疽热

disease *n.* 疾病

bacteria *n.* 细菌

2001. On that day, *terrorists* had killed thousands of people in the United States. Terrorists are people who *frighten* or hurt others to get their way. Now a new terrorist was at work. He or she was sending anthrax letters through the mail. These letters were filled with bacteria. They gave people anthrax. Sixteen people got sick. Three had died.

In each case, police knew what had happened. Some of the sick people were mail workers. The letters had passed through their hands at work. The rest were people who had opened the letters. Either way, it was clear how they got the disease.

Nguyen was a different story. She was not a mail worker. And she had not gotten an anthrax letter. So how did Nguyen get sick? That was the question. Quickly, police went to work to find the answer.

They brought in scientists to test Nguyen's home. There were no

---

千的美国人。恐怖主义者是一群会恐吓或者是伤害任何碍着他们事的人。现在一个新的恐怖主义者正在行动，他（或她）通过邮件寄送炭疽信件。这些信件里都装满了病毒，会让人得上炭疽热。16个人染病，3个死亡。

每个案件中，警察都知道发生了什么。有些染病的人就是邮政人员，他们在工作的时候经手了这些信件。余下的则是打开了这些信的人。不管怎样，他们染病的途径都很清楚。

古颜的情况则不同。她并不是邮政人员，而且她也没有收到炭疽信件。那古颜是怎么染病的呢？这就是问题所在。很快，警察开始寻找答案。

他们找来科学家来检测古颜的家。那里没有炭疽杆菌。之后他们检查

---

terrorist *n.* 恐怖主义者   frighten *v.* 惊恐

anthrax bacteria in it. Next they checked the hospital where she had worked. Nguyen had worked in a room where lots of things were stored. Scientists *checked* the whole room. They found no anthrax bacteria. They ran tests throughout the hospital. Nothing.

They went to the place where Nguyen got her mail. An anthrax letter might have come through there. Bacteria from an anthrax letter could have stuck to a piece of Nguyen's mail. This, too, *turned out* to be a dead end. None of the bacteria showed up at Nguyen's mail center.

Now police were really worried. Had the killer found some new way to spread anthrax? If so, the police had to find it. That was the only way to keep people safe.

Doctors said the bacteria had entered Nguyen's body a few days before she got sick. So police tried to find out what she had done during that time. Where had she gone? How had she spent her time?

了她工作的医院。古颜工作的房间里储存着很多东西。科学家检查了整个房间，却没有找到任何炭疽杆菌。他们检查了整座医院，什么都没有。

他们去了古颜取信的地方，炭疽信可能从那里经过。炭疽信件的病菌可能粘在了古颜的邮件上。这里最终也没有找到结果，在古颜的邮件中心没有发现任何病毒。

现在警察真的开始着急了。是不是杀手找到了新的方法来传播炭疽热呢？如果是这样，警察必须查出来。这是唯一能保证人们安全的办法。

医生说病毒是在古颜生病的前几天进入她的身体的。因此警察开始试着找出她在那段时间干了什么。她去了哪儿？她做了什么？他们询问了古颜的邻居。这些邻居说的都一样。凯西·古颜的生活非常的平静。她住在

---

check *v.* 检查

turn out 结果是

They talked with Nguyen's neighbors. These *neighbors* all said the same thing. Kathy Nguyen led a very quiet life. She had lived next to them for 10 years. She had always been friendly and kind. But she had not gone out much. On Sundays she went to a *church* up the street. And during the week she went to work. That was about it.

"It's not like Kathy traveled a lot or visited a lot of people," said one woman.

A second neighbor agreed. "She was always from her job to her house, from her house to her job. She sometimes said she was tired from working all the time and just wanted to be home."

This was not much help. Still, the police did their best. They checked every place they could think of where she might have been. They checked the stores where she shopped. They checked the place where she washed her clothes. They found out that she had a favorite *restaurant*. They checked it out. They even found out what

---

他们隔壁已经有十年了，她一直都很友好和善，但她很少出门。周日的时候她会去街的另一头的教堂，平时的时候她会去工作。就是这样。

"凯西不常出去旅游或者是拜访很多人。"一个女人说。

下一个邻居对此表示了同意，"她经常是从单位到家，从家到单位。她有时候会说她厌倦了一直工作，她只是想要回家。"

这些没有什么价值，警察仍然尽力而为，他们检查了他们能想到的她会去的每个地方。他们检查了她购物的商店，他们检查了她洗衣服的地方。他们找出了一家她喜欢的餐馆，并仔细检查了一番。他们甚至找

---

neighbor *n.* 邻居
restaurant *n.* 餐馆

church *n.* 教堂

subway line she took to work. They checked each stop between her home and her job. They didn't come up with a thing.

In the end, the police gave up. So did the scientists. They just could not find out where Kathy Nguyen had picked up anthrax.

For a while, not knowing how Nguyen had gotten sick made everyone pretty worried. "It's very scary," said one of Nguyen's friends, "because what happened to her could happen to anyone."

That was true. But Americans were lucky. After Nguyen died, only a few more people came down with anthrax. By the end of 2001, the scare was ending. Police still did not know who had sent the anthrax letters. More *puzzling*, they did not know how Kathy Nguyen got the disease. Maybe someday they will find the answer. For now, though, her case is still *unsolved*.

出了她上班的地铁线。他们检查了她家和单位之间的每个站点，但毫无发现。

最后，警察们放弃了，科学家们也是，他们无法找出凯西·古颜染上炭疽热的原因。

有一段时间，没法知道古颜染病的途径让每个人都很担心。"那非常恐怖，"古颜的一个朋友说，"因为发生在她身上的事可能发生在任何人身上。"

这话没错。但是美国人很幸运。在古颜死后，只有几个人染上了炭疽热。到了2001年年末，恐慌终于结束了，警察仍然不知道是谁寄出的炭疽信件。更莫名其妙的是，他们不知道凯西·古颜是怎样染上此病的。也许有一天他们会找到答案。但到目前，她的案子仍然未解。

---

puzzle *v.* 使困惑   unsolved *adj.* 未解决的

21

Costa Rica's Strange Spheres

The forests of Costa Rica held a secret. But for hundreds of years, no one knew it. People thought these forests were nothing but *jungle*. They thought the jungle only had trees, *vines*, and animals. In fact, the forests did have these things. But they had something else too. They held within them one of the biggest mysteries of all time.

Shown here in front of the National Museum in San Jose, Costa Rica, are some of the strange stone balls that workers found when they went to clear some land in the Costa Rican jungle.

哥斯达黎加的奇怪球体

哥斯达黎加圣何塞的国家博物馆前面，摆放着工人们在哥斯达黎加清理树林时发现的奇怪的石球。

哥斯达黎加有一个秘密，但是几百年来，没有人知道这个秘密。人们认为这些森林只不过是一片树林，认为只是一些高树、藤蔓植物和动物。事实上，森林就应该有这些东西，但是他们还有一些别的东西，森林里有一个历史中最大的一个神秘事物。

jungle *n.* 丛林　　　　　　　　　　　　　vine *n.* 藤本植物

The mystery came to light in the 1930s. That's when a fruit *organization* went to Costa Rica. It planned to plant banana trees. First, though, it had to clear some land. So workers burned large patches of the jungle. When they did, they came across something strange. They found *spheres* of stone lying on the forest floor. Some of these balls were small, the size of baseballs. Others were very big. They were as big as cars. All of them looked perfectly round, and all were *smooth* and shiny.

There were hundreds of these spheres. Many were lying in bunches of 10 or more. These had been set down in a special way. Some were in lines. Some had been put together to make shapes. Some had been set on piles of dirt.

There was no way to tell how old the balls were. Some scientists

---

这个神秘的东西于20世纪30年代暴露于公众，此时正好是水果组织到哥斯达黎加，这个组织打算种植香蕉树。但是他们首先得清理出一些土地，所以工人们烧掉了一大片的树林，他们在烧树林时遇到了一件怪事。他们发现在森林的地面上有石头球，有的石球很小，相当于垒球大小；有的很大，有汽车那么大。所有的球都非常圆，都很光滑、明亮。

这里有几百个这样的石球，很多球都是十个或十几个一堆，这是按特殊的方式摆放在一起，有的排成一排，有的排成不同的形状，有的摆在土堆上。

没有一种办法能够知道这些球有多少年的历史，有些科学家说有400

---

organization *n.* 组织　　　　　　　　　　　　　　sphere *n.* 球体
smooth *adj.* 光滑的

said 400 years. Some said 10,000 years. The best guess was that they were between 1,000 and 2,000 years old. That was the age of pots and other things found nearby. The people who made these balls have long since died away. They left few clues about who they were or how they lived. But one thing is clear. They must have worked very hard to make the stone balls. These people did not have great tools. Yet somehow they knew how to cut beautiful spheres out of stone. Even the biggest balls were well *shaped*. Scientists *measured* them. Each one was almost perfectly round.

The bigger balls were heavy. They were more than 30,000 pounds. So they must have been cut from very large blocks of stone. The blocks did not come from the jungle. This kind of rock was only found in certain spots. The nearest spot was 50 miles away. No one

---

年，而有些科学家说有10,000年。最可能的猜测是它们有1000-2000年，这与在附近发现的陶罐的历史相同，制作这些石球的人早已经死了，他们很少留下关于他们是谁和他们怎样生活的线索。但一点是肯定的，他们在制作这些石球时一定费了很大的努力，这些人没有很好的工具，但无论怎样说，他们知道怎样用石头切成这样漂亮的石球，就是最大的球切得也非常好。科学家们对石球进行了测量，每个球都几乎是最完美的正圆体。

最大的球很重，重三万多磅，所以它一定是由一块很大的石块切割成的，这些石块不是来自这片树林，这种石料只见于某些特定的地方，最近的一个地方也在50英里以外，没有人知道这些石球是怎么样或是为什么搬

---

shape *v.* 形成，塑造　　　　　　　measure *v.* 测量

knows how or why the balls were moved so far.

Were the balls cut by hand? If so, it would have taken many years to finish each one. So maybe early Costa Rican people found an easier way. Perhaps they placed blocks of stone at the bottom of a *cascade*. Water would have pounded the blocks day and night. In time, the water might have worn blocks down into balls.

Or maybe they used fire. They could have built a fire on a block of stone. Then they could have *splashed* cold water on it. Heating and cooling rock this way can help break it down. Of course, there would still have been lots of work to do. People would have had to *hammer* or *rub* each ball until it was smooth and round.

In any case, the people who made the balls clearly had great skill. Yet they did not use this skill to make anything else with stone. They

---

到这么远的地方。

这些球是用手工切成的吗？如果是这样，那得需要很多年才能完成一个球。所以非常可能的是早期的哥斯达黎加人得到了一个比较简单的方法。也许他们把石块放在一个瀑布的正下方，水会不分昼夜地重重地落在石块上，时间久了，水就可能把石块磨成了球形。

也可能他们用的是火，他们可能在一块大石头上生火，然后在上面泼冷水，这样反复加热和冷却会有利于石头的破裂，当然他们还有很多的事情要做。人们需要敲击或擦摩这块大石头，一直把它弄到光滑的球形。

无论是哪种情况，能做出这种石球的人一定有很好的技能，但他们不会用这种技能把石头做成别的东西，他们没有留下大的石头建筑，根本也

---

cascade *n.* 小瀑布
hammer *v.* 敲打

splash *v.* 泼
rub *v.* 摩擦

left behind no large stone buildings. They left no other cut stones at all. Why not? Why did they spend so much time making balls and nothing else?

That raises the most puzzling question of all. Why did people make the balls in the first place? No one knows. Some scientists think the balls were used to point out stars. Some say the balls were placed to show where the sun *rose* and set at different times of year. One story is that the balls marked spots where gold could be found. And some say the balls were kept by people to show how *successful* they were. This last idea may sound funny but it makes some sense. Rich people could have had workers make the stone spheres for them. The richest people would have had the biggest ones.

There are other ideas too. The balls might have been used for farming somehow. They might have been part of some church. They might have been works of art.

没有留下切割后别的石块。为什么不呢？他们为什么花这么多的时间制作石球而不是别的东西呢？

这就提出来一个最令人费解的问题，首先是人们为什么要做这种石球？没有人知道为什么。一些科学家认为，这些球是用来指示恒星的；另一些科学家说这些球放在那里是用来指明一年不同时间太阳升起和落下的位置。有一个说法是，球是用来标记可能找到金子的地方。有些人说，这些球留在这里以表明这些人是多么的成功。最后一种观点听起来好像有些可笑，但还真的有些意义。有钱人会请工人为他们做出一些石球，最有钱的人会做最大的石球。

另外还有其他的设想，这些球可能是用来种田，也可能是教堂的一部分，可能是艺术品。

---

rise *v.* 上升；升起　　　　　　successful *adj.* 成功的

Could it be that the balls weren't made by people at all? Could they have come shooting out of a volcano? Could they have been made by ice during an ice age? During an ice age, ice and snow cover much of Earth. Most scientists say no. They point out that no *volcano* has ever *tossed out* stone balls. And ice did not cover Costa Rica in the last ice age. So it seems that people did make the balls. We just don't know how or why.

Most of the balls found so far have now been moved out of the jungle. Many have been broken. People thought there might be something inside. So they cut them up. There may be more balls hidden in Costa Rica's jungle. Maybe someday they will be found. Even so, we may never learn the secrets behind these strange stone balls.

　　这些球有没有可能不是人类制作的呢？会不会是从火山爆发中喷出来的呢？会不会是在冰河世纪时由冰（撞击）而成的呢？在冰河时代，冰雪覆盖着地球的大部分地区，大多数科学家说不对。他们说没有一个火山喷出石头球的，而且在冰河后期，哥斯达黎加地表上也没有冰。所以这些球非常可能是人类制作的，我们只不过是不知道他们怎么做的这些球，还不知道他们为什么做这些球。

　　现在发现的大多数球，都从树林中搬了出来，很多已经被打碎了，人们认为里面可能有什么东西，所以才把他们切开。在哥斯达黎加的树森中可能还藏有更多的石球，可能有一天会被人们发现。虽然如此，我们可能永远不能了解到这些奇怪的球后面的秘密。

---

volcano　*n.*　火山　　　　　　　　　　　　　　　toss out　扔出

22

The Mysteries of the Maya

No one knows how they did it. The Maya did not have metal tools. They did not have *wheels*. Yet they built fine cities with wide streets and big open parks. They put up huge *temples* with stones that fit together perfectly. And that was not all they did. Although they lived more than 1,000 years ago, the Maya did all kinds of things that would be amazing even today. Why, then, did the Mayan people suddenly disappear?

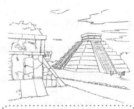

The ruins shown here are all that is left of one Mayan city. A Mayan pyramid can be seen in the top right corner of the picture.

玛雅的神秘故事

这些废墟是玛雅一座城市所留下的一切东西，图片的右上角可见一个玛雅金字塔。

没有人知道他们是怎样做这些事儿的，玛雅人没有金属工具，也没有轮子，但他们建起了很好的城市，有宽敞的街道和开阔的公园。他们用石头建起了巨大的庙宇，而且石头对接完美。他们能做到的还不只是这些，虽然他们生活在1000年以前，但是他们当时做的事情现在看起来还很令人惊讶，那么，为什么玛雅人会突然消失呢？

---

wheel *n.* 轮子   temple *n.* 庙宇

The Maya lived in parts of Mexico and Central America. They were good farmers. They knew how to *drain* low, wet land. They built raised fields where they could plant crops. They cut flat steps into the sides of hills to grow even more crops. And again, they did all this without *metal* tools.

The Maya were great artists. They made wonderful pots, rugs, and necklaces. They wrote books. But perhaps their biggest talent lay in math and science. The Maya studied the sky carefully. They tracked the movement of the stars, the planets, the moon, and the sun. They knew when the sun would be right *overhead*. They knew when one heavenly body would hide another from view. They figured out when Venus would rise in the evening, when it would rise in the morning, and when it would not be seen in the sky.

　　玛雅人住在墨西哥的部分地区和美洲的中部，他们善于种田，他们知道怎样给低湿地排水，他们把农田弄高，在上面种植庄稼，他们在坡地上修起平整的台阶，这样可以种更多的庄稼，而且他们完成这一切都没有金属工具。

　　玛雅人是了不起的艺术家，他们制作出神奇的陶器、毯子和项链，他们写书，但是也许他们最大的天赋表现在数学和科学上。玛雅人对天空研究得很认真，他们跟踪恒星、行星、月亮和太阳的运动，他们知道太阳什么时候正好在头顶，他们知道什么时候一个天体会挡在另一个天体的前面。他们推理出金星在晚上出来的时间，在早晨出来的时间，以及在什么时间里不在天空中出现。

---

drain　*v.*　排水　　　　　　　　　　　　metal　*adj.*　金属制的
overhead　*adv.*　在头顶上

The Maya used this *information* to make calendars. Their *calendars* were outstanding. They went forward and backward in time for half a million years. The Maya had 17 calendars in all. These kept track of all the things they saw happening in the sky. The Maya used a special number system to help them. Our own system is based on the number 10. Theirs was based on the number 20.

And there was one more thing. The Maya knew a great deal about how sound travels. They built a huge open room called the Ball Court. This room was almost 180 feet long. Yet a *whisper* in one end could be heard clearly at the other end. Today's scientists don't know how the Maya were able to build such a thing.

With all their talents, it is no wonder the Maya built such a strong society. What is surprising is that it all came to a screeching halt. In A.D. 800 the Maya seemed to be at the top of their power. But then

---

玛雅人用这些信息建立了日历，他们的日历非常好，向前与向后延展达50万年。玛雅人共有17种日历，他们采用一个特殊的计数系统，我们的计数系统是基于10个数字的，他们的是基于20个数字的。

还有一件事，玛雅人对于声音的传播了解得非常多。他们建起的无房顶的大房子，叫作舞会场，长达180英尺，但是在一端小声说话时，另一端也能听到。今天的科学家们也不知道玛雅人为什么能够建造这种东西。

玛雅人每个人都这样智慧，所以毫不奇怪，他们能建立起如此强大的社会，最令人不解的是他们戛然停止，在公元800年时，玛雅人可能达到了才华的顶峰，这时发生了一件事情，玛雅人不再修建东西了，不再种庄

---

information *n.* 信息　　　　　　　　　　　　calendar *n.* 日历
whisper *n.* 私语

something happened. The Maya stopped building. They stopped planting *crops*. They left their cities. By about 900 the Maya were gone. All they left behind were the ruins of their once-great cities.

No one knows for sure what happened. Some experts think there was fighting between the rich and the poor. A few Mayan leaders were very rich. But most Mayan people were quite poor. The poor people did all the work. Perhaps they got sick of it. They might have killed the leaders. They might have driven the leaders away. Or they might have moved out of the cities themselves. That would have left the leaders with no workers. Any of these things would explain why the Mayan cities suddenly became *deserted*.

Some experts think that war caused the fall of the Maya. It is possible that the great Mayan cities began to fight each other. Wars

---

稼了。他们离开了他们的城市。到了900年时，玛雅人消失了。他们留下的一切只是曾经辉煌城市的废墟。

　　没有人确切地知道发生了什么，一些专家认为富人和穷人发生了战争。玛雅的几个领袖非常有钱，但大多数的玛雅人很穷，穷人要做所有的工作，也许他们开始厌倦工作，他们可能会杀死领袖，他们也可能把领袖赶走，或者他们离开了城市，结果这些领袖没有工人，这一切能够解释为什么玛雅城市突然无人居住。

　　有一些专家认为战争使得玛雅人灭亡了。非常有可能巨大的玛雅城市相互打仗，战争会让大多数人死去，专家们发现一些支持这一观点的线

---

crop *n.* 庄稼　　　　　　　　　　　　deserted *adj.* 荒芜的

may have *wiped out* most of the people. Experts have found clues to back up this idea. They have found burn marks on buildings. They have found *weapons*. They have also found pictures drawn by the Maya showing people at war.

Perhaps lack of rain killed off the Maya. By the 800s the Maya had cut down or burned almost all of their trees. They needed the land for farming. But without trees, much of the soil washed away. It flowed into lakes and *ponds*. Over time, the lakes and ponds filled in and dried up. Of course, the Maya still needed water. So they collected water each time it rained and then stored it. But dry weather would have been a problem. Without rain, the cities would have run out of water. In that case, the Mayan people would have had no choice. They would have had to leave the cities in search of fresh water.

索。他们发现建筑物上有火烧的痕迹，他们找到了武器，他们还发现玛雅人画的图画，表现战争中的人们。

也许是因为缺少雨水而导致了玛雅人的死亡，到公元800年时，玛雅人砍倒或烧光了几乎所有的树。他们需要农田。但是如果没有树，水土流失会变得非常严重，土壤被冲到湖里或水塘里。长期以后，湖或水塘被淤满后变干。当然，玛雅人仍需要水，所以每次下雨时，玛雅人都要把水收集后存起来。但是无雨的天气已经成为问题。没有雨，城里就没有了水，在这种情况下，玛雅人没有别的选择，他们必须离开城市去寻找可饮用水。

wipe out 消灭　　　　　　　　　　　　weapon n. 武器
pond n. 池塘

Or maybe there were just too many people in these cities. Experts believe Mayan cities were very crowded. There may not have been enough food. People may have grown weak. Disease could have spread easily. Bones of Mayan children have been found in the ruins. These bones show the children were smaller than they should have been. So hunger and disease may have wiped out the Mayan cities.

Perhaps all of these things played a role in the fall of the Maya. We just don't know—and we may never *find out*. It may be that the mysteries of the Maya will always be with us. George Stuart puts it best. Stuart is an *expert* on the Maya. He says, "I wake up almost every morning thinking how little we know about the Maya."

另一种可能是，这些城市里的人太多了，专家们认为玛雅人的城市非常拥挤。可能是因为食物不够用，人们变得虚弱，很容易传播疾病。人们在废墟中发现了很多孩子的骨头，这些骨头表明，孩子没有达到应该达到的大小，所以饥饿和疾病可能造成玛雅城市的消失。

也许所有这一切在玛雅灭亡中都起到一定的作用，我们不太清楚，也许我们永远不会找到原因。也可能是玛雅人的神秘将永远与我们同在，乔治·斯图尔特是研究玛雅的专家，他说，"几乎我每天早晨起来时，都在想我们对玛雅的了解是多么少呀。"

---

find out　查明；找出　　　　　　　　　　　　　　　expert　*n.*　专家

23

What Happened to Glen and Bessie Hyde?

Glen and Bessie Hyde had just gotten married. Most couples would have planned to go off on a nice, quiet *honeymoon*. But that was not for Glen and Bessie. They wanted something more. They wanted an *adventure*. And they were willing to face danger to get it.

Shown here is a woman some people believe is Bessie Hyde. This picture was taken after Bessie Hyde disappeared on a rafting trip with her husband. Is she really Bessie Hyde? Nobody knows for sure.

Glen and Bessie decided to raft some rivers. They would start on

格伦和贝西·海德出了什么事情？

图片中为一个女人，一些人认为她是贝西·海德。这张照片是在贝西·海德和丈夫漂流旅行消失后拍的，她是贝西·海德吗？没有人能确定下来。

格伦和贝西·海德刚结完婚，大多数小两口都会计划过一个很好、很安静的蜜月，但对于格伦和贝西却不是这样，他们还要做别的事情，他们想要探险，他们愿意通过面对危险而得到奇遇。

格伦和贝西·海德决定在江河上漂流，他们在犹他州的格林河上出

---

honeymoon *n.* 蜜月   adventure *n.* 探险

the Green River in Utah. Then they would move on to the Colorado River, with its wild *torrents*. Their trip would end hundreds of miles later in California. They knew the journey would be *dangerous*. But Glen, a farmer, loved river boating. And Bessie, an artist, was always ready to try new things.

Glen did have some experience. Two years earlier, he had made a boat trip through Idaho. On that trip, he had spent time with a boat expert. The man had shown Glen how to make a boat by hand. Now Glen had made his own boat. It was in this 20-foot wooden boat that he and Bessie would travel.

The Hydes set out on October 20. They hoped to set three *records*. They wanted to make the fastest trip ever down the Colorado River. If they could do it, they would also be the first ones

---

发，然后他们会到科罗拉多河，这里河流湍急，他们会在加利福尼亚结束旅程，行程为几百英里。他们知道这个旅程是危险的，但是格伦，作为一个农民，热爱在河上划船。而贝西，作为一个艺术家，总喜欢尝试新鲜的事情。

格伦的确有些经验，两年前，他乘船穿过爱达荷州，这次旅行是与一个制船专家一起度过的，这个人告诉格伦如何手工制作船只。这一次格伦自己动手造船，就是乘这条他们造出的20英尺的木船，他和贝西将会一起旅行。

海德夫妇在10月20日出发，他们想创下三个纪录。他们想顺着科罗拉多河作最快的旅行，如果他们能做到这一点，他们也会是最先穿过急流

---

torrent *n.* 奔流   dangerous *adj.* 危险的

record *n.* 最高纪录

to go through every rapid. And Bessie would be the first woman ever to go down the Colorado River.

Things went well at first. Bessie made notes on all the things she saw. She noted each rapid. She wrote about the *twists* and turns in the river. She and Glen had their pictures taken by people they met. They made fast time. In early November, they entered the Grand Canyon. They made it safely through some bad rapids. On November 18, they stopped to eat dinner. They talked with a *sightseer* by the river. But after that, no one saw them again.

A month later, on December 19, their boat was found. It was floating in calm water at the bottom of the Grand Canyon. One of its ropes had caught on a rock. The boat was in perfect shape, and nothing was missing. People found Glen's and Bessie's clothes and hiking boots in the boat, along with a book with maps of the

---

的人，而且贝西也会成为顺流科罗拉多河的第一个女人。

开始时一切都很顺利，贝西把看到的一切都记了下来，她记下了每一个急流，她记下了河中的蜿蜒部分和转弯，她与格伦请遇到的人为他们拍下照片，他们的时间安排得很紧。11月上旬，他们进入了大峡谷，他们安全地通过了几个非常可怕的急流，到了11月18日，他们停下来吃晚饭。他们与一个在河边观光的人交谈，但此后就再没有人看到他们。

一个月后，就在12月19日，人们找到了他们的船，漂在大峡谷脚下的静静的水面上。上面的一条绳子系在岩石上，船没有一点损坏，什么东西都不少，人们在船里发现了格伦和贝西的衣服和旅行鞋，还有一本带这条河地图的书，格伦的枪还留在那里，还有贝西一直记的笔记。船上还有

---

twist n. 急转弯处   sightseer n. 观光者

river. Glen's gun was still there. So were the notes Bessie had been keeping. There was plenty of food *on board* too. In short, everything was there except Glen and Bessie themselves.

People were completely puzzled. They looked for the Hydes for months. They searched the Grand Canyon and the Colorado River, but they found nothing.

What happened to Glen and Bessie? No one knows. But some ideas have been put forward. One is that Bessie killed Glen and then ran away to start a new life. This story spread in 1971. It began when a river guide told sightseers the story of the missing couple. One of the sightseers—an old woman—began to laugh. "I know what happened," she said. "I'm Bessie Hyde." The old woman went on to say that Glen had *treated* her badly. "He was beating me," the old woman said. "I *stabbed* him, threw him in the river, and hiked out."

Was this old woman really Bessie Hyde? And had she really killed

---

很多的食物，简而言之，一切都在船上，就是没有格伦和贝西。

人们被彻底弄懵了，他们用了几个月的时间寻找海德一家，他们找遍了大峡谷和科罗拉多河，但是什么都没有找到。

格伦和贝西出什么事儿了？没有人知道，但是有人提出一些想法，一个是贝西杀死了格伦，然后逃跑了，开始了一个新的生活。这个故事在1971年流传开来，最开始是一个河流向导把这对夫妇丢失的故事讲给了一些观光的人，其中一个观光者是一个老太太，开始笑了。"我知道发生了什么事，"她说，"我就是贝西·海德。"这个老太太接着说道，格伦对她非常不好，"他打我，"这个老太太说，"我用刀捅了他，把他扔进河里，然后就躲了起来。"

这个老太太就是贝西·海德吗？她真的杀死了格伦吗？警察不这样

---

on board 在船上   treat v. 对待
stab v. 刺伤

Glen? The police didn't think so. They never charged her. Many people think the woman made the whole story up, but others are not so sure. They *point out* that the old woman was about as tall as Bessie. Her face looked like Bessie's too. These people wonder if perhaps the old woman was telling the truth.

In 1992 the story of Glen and Bessie took another turn. In that year, a woman named Georgie White died. For years, this woman had lived and boated along the Grand Canyon. But when she died, people learned she wasn't who she'd said she was. Her name wasn't Georgie. It was Bessie. Hidden in one of her dresser drawers was a gun—the same kind of gun the Hydes had carried. Also in the drawer lay a wedding *certificate*. It was made out to Glen and Bessie Hyde.

Was this woman Bessie Hyde? Some people think so. But others do not agree. They point out that river boating was Glen's love, not

---

看。警察也没有起诉她，很多人认为老太太是编出来的故事，但其他人就拿不准了。他们指出这个老太太与贝西身高相同，脸长得也像贝西，这些人猜想，也可能是这个老太太说的是真的。

1992年，格伦和贝西的故事出现了转折点，就在这一年，一个叫乔吉·怀特的女人死了，很多年来，这个女人生活在大峡谷，并总在这里划船。但在她去世的时候，人们了解到她不是她自己所说的那个人，她的名字也不是乔吉，而是贝西。在她的梳妆台的抽屉里有一把枪，正是海德一家带着的那种枪，而且在这个抽屉里还有一个结婚证，是发给格伦和贝西·海德的。

这个女人是贝西·海德吗？一些人认为是的，但另一些人不同意。他

---

point out 指出；指明   certificate *n.* 证书

Bessie's. Why would she have spent her life doing it?

There are other ideas too. Maybe both Glen and Bessie lived through their boat ride. Maybe they wanted a new start in life, so they *faked* a boating accident. They could have hiked out of the canyon and begun new lives with new names someplace else. Or maybe they both drowned. The rapids they had to pass through were very rough. They might both have been washed over the side of the boat. But in that case, why weren't their bodies ever found?

The secret of Glen and Bessie lies in the Grand Canyon. But it is not likely that anyone will find it now. The Hydes had been hoping to set records and win *fame*. They didn't set any records. But they did become famous as the honeymoon couple who never returned.

们指出，格伦喜欢划船，贝西不喜欢，为什么她会用一辈子的时间这样做呢？

还有其他的观点，可能格伦和贝西一直在船上生活，也可能他们想开始一种新的生活，所以他们设计出一个乘船事故。可能他们会徒步走出峡谷，用新的名字在某个地方开始了新的生活。也可能她们两个都淹死了，他们所要穿过的急流是非常可怕的，他们可能会一起被冲下船，如果是这种情况，为什么没有找到他们的尸体呢？

格伦和贝西·海德的秘密藏进了大峡谷，可能不会有人找到他们了。海德一家希望创下纪录，赢得名誉，他们没有创下纪录，但他们在蜜月旅行永远未归这方面还是创下了纪录。

fake *v.* 捏造　　　　　　fame *n.* 名声